AWESOME

Praising God Straight from Scripture

AWESOME

Praising God Straight from Scripture

DAVID GREGORY

ONE
PRESS

Katy, Texas

Awesome: Praising God Straight from Scripture

© 2020 by David Gregory Smith

Cover design by Jun Ares

Interior layout by Sandra Jurca

Published by One Press

Katy, TX

www.davidgregorybooks.com

ISBN 978-0-9675141-4-7

9 8 7 6 5 4 3 2

Printed in the United States of America

Contents

A Journey of Praise.................................vii
How to Use This Book............................ ix
The Praises 1

1st Seven Praises 3
2nd Seven Praises.............................11
3rd Seven Praises 19
4th Seven Praises 27
5th Seven Praises 35
6th Seven Praises 43
7th Seven Praises 51
8th Seven Praises 59
9th Seven Praises 67
10th Seven Praises 75
11th Seven Praises 83
12th Seven Praises 91
13th Seven Praises 99
14th Seven Praises 107
15th Seven Praises 115
16th Seven Praises 123
17th Seven Praises 131
18th Seven Praises 139
19th Seven Praises 147
20th Seven Praises 155

21st Seven Praises. 163

22nd Seven Praises 171

23rd Seven Praises. 179

24th Seven Praises 187

25th Seven Praises. 195

26th Seven Praises. 203

27th Seven Praises. 211

28th Seven Praises. 219

29th Seven Praises. 227

30th Seven Praises. 235

31st Seven Praises. 243

About the Author. 251

Other Books by David Gregory. 252

A Journey of Praise

This book changed my life. I know, that's an odd statement for an author to make. Don't I write books to help other people change *their* lives? Well, the truth is, this didn't start as a book at all. It began as a personal assignment, or invitation, from God.

I was going through a difficult stretch in my life. How difficult? In 2011, I got walking pneumonia and then started coughing up half a cup of blood an hour. For five days. The doctors finally discovered a tumor in my right lung. They had to take out the lower two lobes. I was in the hospital for over two weeks and took months to recover.

All of that was like getting a normal cavity filled at the dentist compared to what was to come. A few years later I lost my marriage, my kids, many of my friends, and all of my money. I was hauled into court four times, lied about, and ruled against. No matter how hard I prayed, my circumstances kept going from bad to worse.

In the midst of it all, the Holy Spirit led me to start praising God regularly. I went through Psalms and marked every part that was a praise to God, and I began saying them out loud to him. Soon, I was doing it multiple times a day.

I went through the entire Bible, pulling out every praise, every thanksgiving, and everything that could easily be turned into a praise or thanksgiving. I used them to do exactly what God told us, to "offer up a sacrifice of praise continually," to "give thanks in everything," even to "give thanks *for* everything." (Yes, Ephesians 5:20 actually says that.)

Honestly, I didn't feel thankful for anything that had happened to me or my children. I couldn't change my feelings.

But I could choose to obey. I could praise God. And I could give thanks, despite my feelings.

I did, and my life changed. Not immediately. Gradually. Until one day I realized that I was giving thanks, and I actually *felt* thankful. Deep inside, regardless of what the circumstances were, I *knew* that God really was working all things together for my good, and the good of my children. I was spontaneously doing another thing God told us to do: rejoice always.

God didn't choose to change my circumstances. But he did an even greater miracle: he changed me. Praising God continually produced in me more joy, more peace, more contentment, more experience of God's love, and more ability to love others than anything else I have ever done.

I guess there's a reason God tells us to continually thank and praise him. Jesus did it. He taught his disciples to do it. The heavenly host do it. Simply put, praising God puts our focus on him instead of on ourselves or our circumstances. And that changes everything.

I think a lot of Christians would love to make praising God a regular part of their lives. But how? We sit down, praise God for everything we can think of, and three minutes have gone by. Now what?

Now there's a resource that provides us with every praise and thanksgiving to God in the Bible, written in the first person, straight to him. No one ever needs to run out of material to praise God with again!

O magnify the LORD with me!
Let's exalt his name together!
PSALM 34:3

How to Use This Book

My best advice is to use this resource however God leads you to. We're not here to perform religious duties. We have the amazing privilege of being the vessels Jesus chooses to live in. He knows how he wants to live through us, and he puts that on our hearts.

If you want to use the book to praise God seven times a day, as David mentioned (Psalm 119), it's set up for that. I've divided all the praises into seven categories, four from the Old Testament, two from the New Testament, and one from both. There are 31 sets of seven one-page praises, enough for a whole month.

If you want to go through each set in a week, there's a praise for each day. Reading one praise out loud to God takes about two minutes.

If you find that certain praises are most meaningful to you and you want to use them over and over, go for it.

If you want to get a group of believers together at your church or online and praise God together, fantastic! What better reason for Christ's Body to get together, than to praise him?

Someone may ask, is everything in these pages really straight from the Scriptures? Yes, absolutely! The Scripture references are listed at the bottom of each page. In the past I have praised God using praises I or others have written *based on* biblical truths. Although I found that profitable, for me, it wasn't as meaningful as praising God using praises that *he himself* has written.

In a few places in the book, verses have been adjusted very slightly for readability and flow. Other than that, they have been changed into first person, so you can read them aloud as a prayer straight to God.

And that, actually, is how I wholeheartedly recommend that they be read—OUT LOUD. God doesn't just want us to silently read praises to him. He wants us to *praise* him. That's the whole purpose of this resource.

Sometimes I've included verses from the Old Testament that are clearly praises for what God has done, or will do, for Israel. In each case, I simply asked, does the Bible make it clear that this applies to believers under the New Covenant as well? If so, I included it.

My prayer for you (and me) is that we will not only take the plunge in praising God, but *stick with it*. The heavens and the earth all praise his glory. We are made to praise God. What better way to do it consistently than praising him through his own Word?

> *My heart is steadfast, God!*
> *I will sing and make melody with all my being!...*
> *I will give thanks to you, O Lord, among the peoples;*
> *I will sing praises to you among the nations.*
> PSALM 108:1, 3, ESV

To him be the glory forever!

THE PRAISES

1st Seven Praises

I will bless the Lord at all times;
his praise will always be in my mouth.
Oh, magnify the Lord with me.
Let's exalt his name together.

PSALM 34:1, 3

The Sovereign Creator of All

In the beginning, God, you created the heavens and the earth.

The earth was formless and empty, and darkness was over the surface of the deep. And you, Holy Spirit, were hovering over the surface of the waters.

God, you said, "Let there be light," and there was light. You saw that the light was good. And you separated the light from the darkness.

You said, "Let there be an expanse in the midst of the waters, and let it separate the waters from the waters." And it was so.

You said, "Let the waters under the sky be gathered together into one place, and let the dry land appear." And it was so.

You said, "Let the earth yield grass, plants yielding seeds, and fruit trees bearing fruit after their kind, with their seeds in it, on the earth." And it was so.

And you saw that it was good.

You said, "Let there be lights in the expanse of the heavens to separate the day from the night. And let them be for signs to mark seasons, days, and years; and let them be for lights in the expanse of the heavens to give light on the earth."

And it was so. You made the two great lights—the greater light to rule the day and the lesser light to rule the night.

You also made the stars. You set them in the expanse of the heavens to give light on the earth, to rule over the day and over the night, and to separate the light from the darkness.

And you saw that it was good.

Sovereign Creator, I praise you!

Genesis 1:1-19

PSALMS

Lord, you are the God of my righteousness.
> I trust in you.
> You have let the light of your face shine on me.
You have put gladness in my heart,
> more than when their grain and their new wine abound.
In peace I will both lay myself down and sleep,
> for you alone, Lord, make me dwell in safety.

Lord, you are my King and my God;
> in the abundance of your lovingkindness I will come
>> to you.
> I will bow in reverence of you.
I take refuge in you and rejoice.
> I shout for joy, because you defend me.
I am joyful in you, because l love your name.
> For you will bless me, the righteous.
You will surround me with favor as with a shield.

Lord, I trust in your lovingkindness.
> My heart rejoices in your salvation.
I will sing to you,
> because you have been good to me.

I remember your name, Lord, in the night.
> At midnight I will rise to give thanks to you.
Lord, you show your marvelous lovingkindness;
> you save me, for by your right hand I take refuge from
>> my enemies.

You keep me as the apple of your eye.
> You hide me under the shadow of your wings.
As for me, I will see your face in righteousness.
> When I awake I will be satisfied with seeing your form.
I thank you, Lord!

PSALM 4:1, 5, 7-8; 5:2, 7, 11-12; 13:5-6; 17:7-8, 15; 119:55, 62

THE LOVING AND FAITHFUL GOD

Lord, you have been my shepherd all my life long to this day. You are the Mighty One. God, you are the one who helps me. You are the Almighty, who blesses me. You bless me with the blessings of heaven.

I will sing to you, Lord, for you have triumphed gloriously.
> You are my strength and my song;
> you have become my salvation.
You are my God, and I will praise you and exalt you.
> I AM THAT I AM is your name.
Your right hand, Lord, is glorious in power;
> your right hand, Lord, dashes the enemy in pieces.
In the greatness of your majesty you overthrow your adversaries;
> you send out your wrath; it consumes them as stubble.
Who is like you, Lord, among the gods?
> Who is like you, majestic in holiness,
> awesome in glorious deeds, doing wonders?
You, in your lovingkindness, have led us whom you have redeemed;
> you have guided us by your strength.
You will reign forever and ever.
> I will sing to you, Lord, for you have triumphed gloriously.

Lord, you are my banner. You are my God. You are merciful and gracious, slow to anger, and abundant in lovingkindness and faithfulness. Your presence goes with me, and you give me rest.

You are God. You are holy. You make me holy.

You bless me and keep me.
> You make your face shine on me
> and are gracious to me.
You lift up your face toward me,
> and give me peace.

GENESIS 22:14; 48:15; 49:24-25; EXODUS 15:1-2, 6-7, 11, 13, 18, 21;
EXODUS 17:15; 29:46; 33:14; 34:6; LEVITICUS 11:44-45; 22:32; NUMBERS 6:24-26

FATHER, SON, SPIRIT

Father, love is of you, for you are love.

You so loved the world, that you gave your one and only Son, that whoever believes in him should not perish, but have eternal life.

Your love was revealed in me by this, that you sent your one and only Son into the world that I might live through him.

In this is love, not that I loved you, God, but that you loved me, and sent your Son as the atoning sacrifice for my sins.

You showed your love toward me in that, while I was still a sinner, Christ died for me.

You are love.

Jesus, you love me. You gave yourself up for me, an offering and a sacrifice to God.

Greater love has no one than this, that someone lay down his life for his friends. You have laid down your life for me. You have called me your friend.

Your perfect love, Father, casts out fear.

I love you, because you first loved me.

I am loved by you and chosen by you.

You chose me from the beginning for salvation, so I could obtain the glory of my Lord Jesus Christ.

Father, you are love.

Your love, the grace of Jesus, and the fellowship of the Holy Spirit are with me.

I praise you!

JOHN 15:13-15; ROMANS 5:8; 2 CORINTHIANS 13:14; EPHESIANS 5:2;
1 THESSALONIANS 1:4; 2 THESSALONIANS 2:13-14, 16; 1 JOHN 4:7-10, 17-19

CHRIST'S VICTORY

Jesus, you are image of the invisible God. You are the radiance of God's glory, the exact representation of his nature.

The Father was pleased for all of his fullness to dwell in you.

In your face is the glory of God.

You became flesh, Jesus, and lived among us. People saw your glory, the glory of the one and only Son of the Father, full of grace and truth.

From your fullness we have all received, and grace upon grace. The law was given through Moses. Grace and truth were realized through you, Jesus.

No one has seen God at any time. You, the one and only Son, who are in the bosom of the Father, you have revealed him.

Whoever sees you, sees the Father. Whoever knows you, knows the Father.

In you all the fullness of Deity dwells in bodily form.

Jesus, you revealed the Father to those he gave you out of the world.

Whoever believes in you, believes not in you, but in him who sent you.

Whoever saw you saw him who sent you. You came as a light into the world, that whoever believes in you may not remain in the darkness.

I praise you, Lord!

JOHN 1:14-18; 12:44-46; 14:7-9; 2 CORINTHIANS 4:4, 6; COLOSSIANS 1:15, 19; 2:9; HEBREWS 1:3

Psalms

Lord, my God, I take refuge in you.
    You administer justice to the peoples.
My shield is with you, God.
    You are a righteous judge.
I will give thanks to you according to your righteousness,
    and will sing praise to your name, O God Most High.

Lord, you are King forever and ever!
    You have heard the desire of the humble.
    You will strengthen their heart.
You will cause your ear to hear,
    to vindicate the fatherless and the oppressed,
    that man who is of the earth may terrify no more.

In you, Lord, I take refuge.
    You are in your holy temple;
    you are on your throne in heaven.
Your eyes observe;
    your eyes examine the children of men.
You examine the righteous,
    for you are righteous.
You love righteousness.
    The upright will see your face.

Lord, your words are flawless words,
    as silver refined in a clay furnace, purified seven times.
You will keep them, Lord.
    You will preserve them from this generation forever.

I will triumph in your salvation.
    In the name of my God, I will set up my banners.
You will answer me from your holy heaven,
    with the saving strength of your right hand.
Some trust in chariots, and some in horses,
    but I trust your name, O Lord my God.

Psalm 7:1, 8, 10-11, 17; 10:16-18; 11:1, 4-5, 7; 12:6-7; 20:5-7

THINGS TO COME

Jesus, you are the shoot that came out of the stock of Jesse,
    a branch out of Jesse's roots to bear fruit.
God's Spirit rested on you:
    the spirit of wisdom and understanding,
    the spirit of counsel and might,
    the spirit of knowledge and of the fear of God.
Your delight is in obeying God.
You will not judge by appearances,
    or decide by the hearing of your ears;
But you will judge the poor with righteousness,
    and decide with equity for the humble of the earth.
You will strike the earth with the rod of your mouth;
    and with the breath of your lips you will kill the wicked.
Righteousness and faithfulness will be the belt of your waist.
The wolf will live with the lamb,
    and the leopard will lie down with the young goat,
    the calf, the young lion, and the fattened calf together;
    and a little child will lead them.
The cow and the bear will graze.
    Their young ones will lie down together.
    The lion will eat straw like the ox.
The nursing child will play near a cobra's hole,
    and the weaned child will put his hand on the viper's den.
They will not hurt nor destroy in all your holy mountain;
    for the earth will be full of the knowledge of God,
    as the waters cover the sea.
In that day the nations will seek you.
You will be as a banner of the peoples;
    and your resting place will be glorious.

Jesus, I praise you!

ISAIAH 11:1-10

2ND SEVEN PRAISES

My heart is steadfast, God!
I will sing and I will make music with my soul.
I will wake up the dawn!
I will give thanks to you, Lord, among the nations.
I will sing praises to you among the peoples.
Be exalted, God, above the heavens!
Let your glory be over all the earth!

PSALM 108:1-3, 5

THE SOVEREIGN CREATOR OF ALL

God, you said, "Let the waters swarm with living creatures, and let birds fly above the earth in the open expanse of the sky."

So you created the great sea creatures and every living creature that moves, with which the waters swarmed, after their kind, and every winged bird after their kind.

And you saw that it was good.

And you blessed them, saying, "Be fruitful and multiply and fill the waters in the seas, and let birds multiply on the earth."

You said, "Let the earth produce living creatures after their kind—livestock, creeping things, and animals of the earth after their kind." And it was so.

And you saw that it was good.

Then you said, "Let us make man in our image, after our likeness. Let them have dominion over the fish of the sea, and over the birds of the sky, and over the livestock, and over all the earth and over every creeping thing that creeps on the earth."

So you created man in your own image, in the image of God you created him; male and female you created them.

You blessed them and said to them, "Be fruitful, multiply, fill the earth, and subdue it. Have dominion over the fish of the sea, over the birds of the sky, and over every living thing that moves on the earth."

And you saw everything that you had made, God, and it was very good.

Sovereign Creator, I praise you!

GENESIS 1:20-27

PSALMS

Lord, my Lord, how majestic is your name in all the earth!
> You have set your glory above the heavens!

From the lips of babes and infants you have established
> strength,
>> because of your adversaries,
>> that you might silence the enemy and the avenger.

When I consider your heavens, the work of your fingers,
> the moon and the stars, which you have ordained;

What is man, that you think of him?
> What is the son of man, that you care for him?

For you have made him a little lower than the angels,
> and crowned him with glory and honor.

You make him ruler over the works of your hands.
> You have put all things under his feet.

Lord, my Lord, how majestic is your name in all the earth!

I will give thanks to you, Lord, with my whole heart.
> I will tell of all your marvelous works.

I will be glad and rejoice in you.
> I will sing praise to your name, O Most High.

You sit on the throne judging righteously.
> You reign forever.
> You have prepared your throne for judgment.

You will judge the world in righteousness.
> You will administer judgment to the peoples in
> uprightness.

Lord, you will also be a high tower for the oppressed,
> a high tower in times of trouble.

Those who know your name will put their trust in you,
> for you, Lord, have not forsaken those who seek you.

I sing praises to you,
> and declare among the people what you have done.
> I will rejoice in your salvation.

You have made yourself known.
> You have executed judgment.

The needy will not always be forgotten,
> nor the hope of the poor perish forever.

PSALM 8:1-6, 9; 9:1-4, 7-11, 14, 16, 18

THE LOVING AND FAITHFUL GOD

I praise you, Lord! I lift up my hand to you. You are the Lord who provides.

You are God Almighty. You said to Abraham:

> "I will make of you a great nation. I will bless you and make your name great. All the families of the earth will be blessed through you."

You said to him:

> "I will establish my covenant between me and you and your offspring after you throughout their generations. It will be an everlasting covenant, to be God to you and to your offspring after you. I am your shield, your exceedingly great reward."

You are not man, that you should lie,
    or a son of man,
    that you should change your mind.
You have said it, and will you not do it?
    You have spoken, and will you not make it good?
    You have blessed; you are with me.
Lord, I will proclaim your name.
    I will ascribe greatness to you!
My Rock: your work is perfect,
    for all your ways are just.
A God of faithfulness who does no wrong,
    just and right are you.
You have made and established me.
    Your people are your portion.
You surround me; you care for me.
    You keep me as the apple of your eye.
As an eagle that stirs up her nest,
    that flutters over her young,
You spread your wings over me,
    you take me and bear me on your feathers.
You alone do this.

I praise you, Lord!

GENESIS 12:2-3; 17:1, 7-8; 15:1; NUMBERS 23:19-21; DEUTERONOMY 32:3-4, 6, 8-12

FATHER, SON, SPIRIT

Father, you love the Son. He is in your bosom. I am in him.

You love me, even as you love Jesus.

The love you have for him, you have put in me. Your love has been poured into my heart through the Spirit who was given to me.

Jesus, the Father loved you before the foundation of the world. Just as the Father loved you, so you have loved me.

You love the Church, your body. You gave yourself up for me, that you might sanctify me, having cleansed me by the washing of water with the word.

You did this to present me to yourself gloriously, without spot or wrinkle or any such thing, so I would be holy and without defect.

Jesus, you nourish and cherish me, because I am a member of your body, of your flesh and bones.

I belong to you. I am beloved of God.

Father, I know and have believed the love which you have for me.

If you are for me, who can be against me? You didn't spare your own Son, but delivered him up for me. How will you not also with Jesus freely give me all things?

Who could possibly separate me from your love? Could oppression, or anguish, or persecution, or famine, or nakedness, or peril, or sword? Even in all these things, I am more than a conqueror through you who loved me.

I know that neither death, nor life, nor angels, nor princi-palities, nor things present, nor things to come, nor powers, nor height, nor depth, nor any other created thing will be able to separate me from your love, Father, which is in Jesus.

JOHN 1:18; 15:9; 17:21, 23, 24, 26; ROMANS 1:7; 5:5; 8:31-32, 35-39; EPHESIANS 5:25-27, 29-30; 1 JOHN 4:16

CHRIST'S VICTORY

Father, you are blessed.

You prepared your salvation before the face of all peoples;
    a light for revelation to the nations,
    and the glory of your people Israel.

Jesus, the Holy Spirit came upon Mary, and the power of the
Most High overshadowed her. Therefore you, the Holy One,
were born from her, and called the Son of God. For nothing
is impossible with God.

The virgin was with child,
    and gave birth to a son.
They called your name Immanuel,
    which means "God with us."

You were conceived of the Holy Spirit. You were named Jesus,
for you were the one to save your people from their sins.

Father, your glory shone, and you announced good news of
great joy for all people. There was born for me, in David's
city, a Savior, Christ the Lord.

A multitude of the heavenly army praised you, Father, saying,

"Glory to God in the highest,
    on earth peace, good will toward men."

Jesus, you were born King of the Jews. As the prophet
Micah said, "Out of Bethlehem shall come a ruler who will
shepherd my people, Israel." Wise men from the east saw
your star and came to worship you. I worship you!

Father, every mountain and hill was brought low.
    The crooked became straight,
    and the rough ways smooth.
All flesh saw your salvation in Jesus.

MATTHEW 1:20, 23; 2:1-2, 6; LUKE 1:34-37; 2:9-14, 28-33; 3:5-6

Psalms

Lord, why do the nations rage,
 and the peoples plot a vain thing?
The kings of the earth take a stand,
 and the rulers take counsel together,
 against you, God, and against your Anointed, saying,
"Let's break their bonds apart,
 and cast their cords from us."
You who sit in the heavens laugh.
 You scoff at them.
You will speak to them in your anger,
 and terrify them in your wrath:
"I have set my King on my holy hill of Zion.
 I have said to him:

 'You are my son.
  Today I have become your father.
 Ask of me, and I will give the nations for your inheritance,
  the uttermost parts of the earth for your possession.
 You will break them with a rod of iron.
  You will dash them in pieces like a potter's vessel.'"

Blessed are all those who take refuge in you, Lord.
 You are a shield around me,
 my glory, and the one who lifts up my head.
I cry to you with my voice,
 and you answer me.
I lay myself down and sleep.
 I awake, for you sustain me.
I will not be afraid of tens of thousands of people
 who have set themselves against me on every side.
Salvation belongs to you, Lord.
 Your blessing is on me.

I praise you!

Psalm 2:1-9, 12; 3:1, 4-8

THINGS TO COME

Lord, in your mountain you will destroy the shroud that covers all peoples, the veil that is spread over all nations. You will swallow up death forever!

You will wipe away tears from every face. You will take the reproach of your people away from all the earth.

You have spoken it. In that day it will be said,

> "Behold, this is our God! We have waited for him, and he will save us! This is the Lord! We have waited for him. We will be glad and rejoice in his salvation!"

You will come as a mighty one, Lord,
and your arm will rule for you.

Your reward will be with you,
and your recompense before you.

You will feed your flock like a shepherd.
You will gather the lambs in your arm,
and carry them in your bosom.
You will gently lead those who have their young.

Lord, the sun will no longer be my light by day;
nor will the brightness of the moon give light to me,
But you will be my everlasting light,
and my God will be my glory.
The sun will not go down any more,
nor will the moon withdraw itself;
For you will be my everlasting light,
and the days of my sorrow will end.

Lord, I praise you!

ISAIAH 25:7-9; 40:10-11; 60:19-20

3RD SEVEN PRAISES

Through [Christ] then, let's offer up
a sacrifice of praise to God continually,
that is, the fruit of lips that give thanks to
his name.

HEBREWS 13:15

THE SOVEREIGN CREATOR OF ALL

Blessed be you, God Most High. You are the possessor of heaven and earth.

Lord, you are God. You are holy. You are a consuming fire.

Lord, you are God. You are one. You are I AM THAT I AM. That is your name forever.

You are the Lord, the God of heaven and earth. Blessed be you, Lord. I worship you. You are God Almighty.

O Lord, you are great, with a mighty hand. What God is there in heaven or on earth that can do works like yours, and mighty acts like yours?

You created man on the earth, and made one end of the sky to another. You are God. There is no one else besides you. You are God in heaven above and on earth beneath.

You are a great and awesome God. I consider your greatness, your mighty hand and your outstretched arm.

To you, Lord, belong heaven, the heaven of heavens, and the earth, with all that is in it. You are the God of gods and Lord of lords, the great God, the mighty, and the awesome.

You are judge of all the earth. All the earth is yours. You are a warrior. I AM THAT I AM is your name.

You execute justice for the fatherless and the widow and love the foreigner.

You are my praise, and you are my God. You have done great and awesome things for me. My eyes have seen all the great work you have done. Before all the people you will be glorified.

GENESIS 14:18-19; 18:25; 24:3, 26-27; 35:11; EXODUS 3:14-15; 15:3; 19:5; LEVITICUS 10:3; 11:44; DEUTERONOMY 3:24; 4:24, 32, 35, 39; 6:4; 7:21; 10:14, 17-21; 11:2, 7

PSALMS

I take refuge in you, God.
You are my Lord.
> Apart from you I have no good thing.
You assigned my portion and my cup.
> You made my lot secure.
I will bless you, Lord, who have given me counsel.
> My heart instructs me in the night seasons.
I have set you always before me.
> Because you are at my right hand, I will not be moved.
Therefore my heart is glad, and my tongue rejoices.
> My body will also dwell in safety.
For you will not leave my soul in Sheol,
> neither will you allow your holy one to see decay.
You will show me the path of life.
> In your presence is fullness of joy.
In your right hand there are pleasures forevermore.

Lord, you are my light and my salvation.
> Whom shall I fear?
You are the strength of my life.
> Of whom shall I be afraid?
One thing I have asked of you, that I will seek:
> that I may dwell with you all the days of my life,
> to see your beauty, and to inquire of you.
For in the day of trouble, you will keep me secretly in
> your pavilion.
> In the secret place you will hide me.
You will lift me up on a rock.
> You have lifted my head above my enemies.
I will offer sacrifices of joy.
> I will sing, yes, I will sing praises to you.
When you said, "Seek my face,"
> my heart said to you, "I will seek your face, Lord."
You are my help; you are the God of my salvation.
> I am confident of this:
> I will see your goodness in the land of the living.

PSALM 16:1-2, 5, 7-11; 27:1, 4-6, 8-9, 13

THE LOVING AND FAITHFUL GOD

Lord, you have redeemed me.

You have blessed me, because you love me.

You are the one who goes with me. You will not fail me or forsake me.

Lord, you are the God who made us,
 The Rock of our salvation.
You are my Father,
 The God who gave me birth.

You love me. I am in your hand.
 You direct me.

Lord, I am your beloved. Because of you I dwell in safety. You cover me all day long. You dwell between my shoulders.

I am saved by you. You are the shield for my help, the sword of my triumph. Your enemies will submit themselves to you, and you will tread on their high places.

Lord, you are the faithful God who keeps covenant and lovingkindness with those who love you.

I know in my heart and in my soul that not one thing fails of all the good things which you speak. All of it happens. Not one thing fails.

Lord, you are with me wherever I go.

I have seen all that you have done for me.

You are the one who has fought for me, just as you promised.

You are my God.

DEUTERONOMY 7:9; 15:15; 23:5; 31:6; 32:15, 18; 33:3, 12, 29; JOSHUA 1:9; 23:3, 10, 14; 24:18

FATHER, SON, SPIRIT

Jesus, you are the Word. In the beginning, you were. You were with God, and you were God. All things were made through you.

In you is life, and the life is the light of men. You, the light, shine in the darkness, and the darkness has not overcome it. You are the true light that enlightens everyone.

You are the Lamb of God, who takes away the sin of the world.

You are the Son of God and the Son of Man. You are the Messiah, the King of Israel. You are the Christ, the Savior of the world.

You are the bread of life. Whoever comes to you will not hunger, and whoever believes in you will never thirst.

You are the light of the world. Whoever follows you will not walk in darkness, but will have the light of life.

You are the door for the sheep. Anyone who enters by you will be saved. You came that I might have abundant life.

You are the good shepherd. The good shepherd lays down his life for the sheep.

You are the resurrection and the life. Whoever lives and believes in you will never die.

You are the way, the truth, and the life. No one comes to the Father, except through you.

You are the true vine. I am a branch in you. Apart from you I can't do anything.

God appointed you heir of all things. Through you he made the world. You uphold all things by the word of your power.

You are my Lord and my God.

You are the Christ, the Son of the living God. I have believed you, and I have life in your name.

JOHN 1:1-5, 9, 29, 35, 49; 3:13; 4:42; 6:35; 8:12; 10:9-11; 11:25-26; 13:13; 14:6; 15:1-5; 20:28, 31; HEBREWS 1:2-3

CHRIST'S VICTORY

Jesus, the Spirit of the Lord was upon you,
    because he anointed you to preach good news to the poor.
He sent you to heal the brokenhearted,
    to proclaim release to the captives,
    recovery of sight to the blind,
    to deliver those who were crushed,
    and to proclaim the acceptable year of the Lord.

Jesus, you began to perform your signs in Cana, and you
revealed your glory.

God anointed you with the Holy Spirit and with power. You
went about doing good and healing all who were oppressed
by the devil.

People from every region came to hear you and to be healed
of their diseases, and those troubled by unclean spirits, and
they were healed. All the multitude sought to touch you, for
power came out of you and healed them all.

All those who were sick with various diseases were brought
to you, and you laid your hands on every one of them, and
healed them, that what was spoken through Isaiah would be
fulfilled: "He took our infirmities and bore our diseases."

You cast out the spirits with a word. Demons came out of
many, crying out, "You are the Christ, the Son of God!"

Because of you, the blind received their sight, the lame walked,
the lepers were cleansed, the deaf heard, the dead were raised
up, and the poor had good news preached to them.

All the people were astonished at the majesty of God. They
marveled at all the things you did. Amazement took hold on
all the people, and they glorified God.

You commanded even the wind and the water, and they
obeyed you.

Jesus, I praise you!

MATTHEW 8:16-17; LUKE 4:18-19, 40-41; 5:26; 6:17-19; 7:22; 8:25; 9:42-43;
JOHN 2:11; ACTS 10:38

PSALMS

I love you, O Lord, my strength.
You are my rock, my fortress, and my deliverer;
    my God, my rock, in whom I take refuge;
    my shield, and the horn of my salvation, my high tower.
I call on you, who are worthy to be praised,
    and I am saved from my enemies.
You delivered me from my strong enemy;
    you were my support.
You brought me out into a large place.
    You delivered me, because you delighted in me.
You will light my lamp, Lord.
    My God will light up my darkness.
For by you, I advance through a troop.
    By my God, I leap over a wall.
As for you, God, your way is perfect.
    Your word is tried.
    You are a shield to all those who take refuge in you.
For who is God, except the Lord?
    Who is a rock, besides you, my God,
    the God who arms me with strength, and makes my
        way perfect?
You make my feet like deer's feet,
    and set me on my high places.
You teach my hands to battle,
    so that my arms bend a bow of bronze.
You have also given me the shield of your salvation.
    Your right hand sustains me.
You have enlarged my steps under me;
    my feet have not slipped.
Lord, you live! Blessed be my rock.
    Exalted be the God of my salvation.
    You rescue me from my enemies.
Therefore I will give thanks to you, Lord, among the nations,
    and will sing praises to your name.
You give great deliverance to me,
    and show me lovingkindness forevermore.

PSALM 18:1-3, 17-19, 28-36, 46, 48-50

THINGS TO COME

Lord, you will issue a decree,
  and you will establish your justice for a light to the peoples.
Your righteousness is near.
    Your salvation has gone forth,
    and your arms will judge the peoples.
I lift up my eyes to the heavens,
    and look at the earth beneath;
For the heavens will vanish away like smoke,
    and the earth will wear out like a garment.
Its inhabitants will die in the same way,
    but your salvation will be forever,
    and your righteousness will never fade.
Your people will know righteousness,
    the people in whose heart is your law.
For your righteousness will be forever,
    and your salvation to all generations.

Lord, you will save Israel out of all their dwelling places and
        will cleanse them.
They will be your people, and you will be their God.

Your servant David will be king over them. They all will
have one shepherd. They will dwell in the land you gave to
Jacob, they, and their children, and their children's children,
forever. David your servant will be their prince forever.

You will make a covenant of peace with them, an everlasting
covenant. You will set your sanctuary among them forevermore.
You will be their God, and they will be your people.

The nations will know that you are the Lord who sanctifies
Israel, when your sanctuary is among them forevermore.

Lord, I praise you!

ISAIAH 51:4-8; EZEKIEL 37:23-28

4TH SEVEN PRAISES

Praise the Lord!
Praise, you servants of the Lord,
praise the name of the Lord.
Blessed be the name of the Lord
from this time forth and forevermore!
From the rising of the sun to its going down,
the name of the Lord is to be praised!

PSALM 113:1-3

THE SOVEREIGN CREATOR OF ALL

Lord, you are the God of the spirits of all people.

All the earth will be filled with your glory.

You are my life and length of days.

Lord, you are the One.
     There is no god besides you.

You kill and make alive.
     You wound and heal.
     There is no one who can deliver out of your hand.

There is none like you, God,
     who rides on the heavens to help me,
     through the skies in your majesty.

You, the eternal God, are my dwelling place;
     underneath me are your everlasting arms.

You are God in the heavens above and on the earth beneath.
Your glory fills your temple.

Lord, it is not by strength and not by power, but by your
Spirit. You are the God of the heavenly armies.

You are a great King. You rule over all. Your name is awesome
among the nations.

You are my Father. You are the one who created me.

You, O Lord, do not change.

You are the Lord my God. You are God in heaven above, and
on earth beneath. You are the Mighty One, God—the Lord!
The Mighty One, God—the Lord!

NUMBERS 16:22; 19:21; DEUTERONOMY 30:20; 32:39; 33:26-27; JOSHUA 2:11;
22:22; EZEKIEL 44:4; ZECHARIAH 4:6; MALACHI 1:14; 2:10; 3:6

PSALMS

The heavens declare your glory, God.
> The expanse shows your handiwork.
Day after day they pour out speech,
> and night after night they display knowledge.
There is no speech nor language
> where their voice is not heard.
Their voice has gone out through all the earth,
> their words to the end of the world.
In them you have set a tent for the sun,
> like a bridegroom coming out of his room,
> like a strong man rejoicing to run his course.
Its rising is from one end of the heavens, its path to the other.
> There is nothing hidden from its heat.
Lord, you are my rock and my redeemer.
> I will triumph in your salvation.
> In the name of my God, I will set up my banner.
You save me, your anointed.
> You will answer me from your holy heaven
> with the saving strength of your right hand.
Some trust in chariots, and some in horses,
> but I trust in your name, Lord God.
I rejoice in your strength, Lord!
> How greatly I rejoice in your salvation!
You have given me my heart's desire,
> and have not withheld the request of my lips.
For you meet me with the blessings of goodness.
> My glory is great in your salvation.
> You lay honor and majesty on me.
For you make me most blessed forever.
> You make me glad with joy in your presence,
> for I trust in you.
Through your lovingkindness, Most High,
> I will not be moved.
Be exalted, Lord, in your strength;
> I will sing and praise your power.

PSALM 19:1-6, 14; 20:5-7; 21:1-3, 5-7, 13

THE LOVING AND FAITHFUL GOD

I bless you, Lord!
I will recount your righteous acts,
    the righteous acts of your rule.
You are peace.

Lord, you are God. Under your wings I have come to
take refuge.

Blessed be you, Lord! May your name be famous.

You fulfill all the promises that you have made to me; not
one of them fails. Not one word of all the good promises
that you made to the house of Israel failed; all came to pass.

My heart exults in you, LORD;
    my horn is exalted in you.
My mouth is enlarged over my enemies,
    because I rejoice in your salvation.
There is none holy like you, Lord;
    there is none besides you;
    there is no rock like my God.

Lord, you will not forsake your people, for your great name's
sake. You were pleased to make you a people for yourself.

There is no one besides you to help, between the mighty
and him who has no strength. I rely on you. You are my
God. No man will prevail against you.

I give you thanks, Lord, for your lovingkindness endures
forever.

Father, you have established the kingdom of the Son. You
have established it forever. Your lovingkindness never
departs from him. His throne is established forever.

Lord, you are God. You are the Lord God of hosts. Your
words are truth. Let your name be magnified forever.

JUDGES 5:9-11; 6:24; RUTH 2:12; 4:14; 1 SAMUEL 2:1-2; 12:22; 2 SAMUEL 7:12-16;
25-28; 2 CHRONICLES 14:11; 20:21

FATHER, SON, SPIRIT

Father, you are perfect.

You are my heavenly Father.
May your name be kept holy.
Let your kingdom come.
Let your will be done on earth as it is in heaven.
For yours is the kingdom, the power, and the glory forever.

You are the Most High. You are kind even toward the
unthankful and evil. You are merciful. You make your sun rise
on the evil and the good, and you send rain on both the just
and the unjust.

You feed the birds of the sky. You clothe the grass of the
field. How much more will you clothe me?

You give good things to those who ask you.

It is your good pleasure to give me the kingdom. Your
kingdom is within me.

Thank you, Father, Lord of heaven and earth, that you
have hidden things from the wise and understanding, and
revealed them to little children. This pleased you.

You delivered all things to Jesus, your Son. No one knows
you, except the Son and whomever the Son desires to reveal
you. Father, you reveal to us who Jesus is.

You are the God of Abraham, and the God of Isaac, and the
God of Jacob. You are not the God of the dead, but of the
living, for all are alive to you.

I praise you that the things which are impossible with men
are possible with you. All things are possible with you.

Father, you are God. You are one. You are my Abba.

MATTHEW 5:45, 48; 6:9-10, 26, 30; 7:11; 11:25-27; 16:17; 19:26; 21:42; 22:32;
MARK 10:27; 12:29; 14:36; LUKE 6:35-36; 12:32; 17:21; 18:27; 20:37-38

CHRIST'S VICTORY

Jesus, though you existed in the form of God, you didn't consider equality with God a thing to be grasped.

You emptied yourself, taking the form of a bond-servant, being made in the likeness of men.

In human form, you humbled yourself, becoming obedient to the point of death, even death on the cross.

Therefore God highly exalted you, Jesus, and gave you the name which is above every name, that at the name of Jesus every knee should bow—those in heaven, those on earth, and those under the earth—and that every tongue should confess that you are Lord, to the glory of God the Father.

Jesus, all things written in the law of Moses, the prophets, and the psalms, concerning you had to be fulfilled. You had to suffer and rise from the dead the third day, so that repentance and forgiveness of sins would be preached in your name to all the nations.

You had to suffer many things and be rejected by your generation.

As you broke the bread and gave it to the disciples, you said, "This is my body, which is broken for you." You took the cup and said, "This is my blood of the new covenant, which is poured out for many for the forgiveness of sins."

Your blood was poured out for me. Your body was given for me.

Jesus, you suffered outside the gate, that you might sanctify me through your own blood.

You didn't please yourself, but the reproaches of those who reproached God fell on you.

You suffered for sins once for all, the righteous for the unrighteous, that you might bring me to God. You were put to death in the flesh, but made alive in the Spirit.

I praise you!

MATTHEW 26:26-28; LUKE 17:25; 22:19-20; 24:44-47; ROMANS 15:3;
1 CORINTHIANS 11:24-25; PHILIPPIANS 2:5-11; HEBREWS 13:10; 1 PETER 3:18

PSALMS

Lord, you are holy;
> you inhabit my praises.
I will declare your name to my brothers.
> Among the assembly, I will praise you.
You who fear the Lord, praise him!
> Stand in awe of him!
I praise you in the great assembly.
> Those who seek after you will praise you, Lord.
All the ends of the earth will remember and turn to you.
> All the families of the nations will worship before you.
For the kingdom is yours, Lord.
> You are the ruler over the nations.
All the rich ones of the earth will eat and worship.
> All those who go down to the dust will bow before you.
Posterity will serve you.
> Future generations will be told about you.
They will declare your righteousness to a people that will
> be born,
> for you have done it.

The earth is yours, Lord, with its fullness;
> the world, and those who dwell in it.
For you have founded it on the seas,
> and established it on the floods.
Lift up your heads, you gates!
> Be lifted up, you everlasting doors,
> and the King of glory will come in.
Who is the King of glory?
> You, Lord, strong and mighty,
> you, Lord, mighty in battle.
Lift up your heads, you gates;
> yes, lift them up, you everlasting doors,
> and the King of glory will come in.
Who is this King of glory?
> Lord of hosts, you are the King of glory!

PSALM 22:3, 22-23, 25, 26-31; 24:1-2, 7-10

THINGS TO COME

Lord, you will create new heavens and a new earth.
    The former things will not be remembered,
    nor come into mind.
You will be glad and rejoice forever in that which you create;
    you will create Jerusalem to be a delight,
    and her people a joy.
You yourself will rejoice in Jerusalem,
    and delight in its people;
And the voice of weeping and the voice of crying
    will be heard in her no more.
No more will there be an infant who only lives a few days,
    nor an old man who has not filled his days.
They will build houses and inhabit them.
    They will plant vineyards and eat their fruit.
They will not build and another inhabit.
    They will not plant and another eat:
For the days of its people will be like the days of a tree,
    and your chosen ones will long enjoy the work of
        their hands.
They will not labor in vain
    nor give birth for calamity;
For you will bless their children and
    their descendants after them.
It will happen that before they call, you will answer;
    and while they are yet speaking, you will hear.
The wolf and the lamb will feed together.
    The lion will eat straw like the ox.
    Dust will be the snake's food.
They will not hurt nor destroy in all your holy mountain.
As the new heavens and the new earth, which you will make,
    will remain before you,
    so your offspring and your name will remain.
From one new moon to another, and from one Sabbath
        to another,
    all flesh will come to worship before you.

ISAIAH 65:17-25; 66:22-23

5TH SEVEN PRAISES

My lips will praise you!
So I will bless you while I live.
I will lift up my hands in your name.
My mouth will praise you with joyful lips.

PSALM 63:3-5

THE SOVEREIGN CREATOR OF ALL

I bless you, Lord; to you I will sing;
  I will sing praise to you, my God.
The earth trembles and the skies drop,
  yes, the clouds drop water.
The mountains quake before your presence, LORD.
In your hand is the life of every living thing,
  and the breath of all mankind.

You dried up the waters of the Jordan River and the Red Sea
until your people crossed over, that all the peoples of the
earth may know that your hand is mighty, and that you may
be revered forever.

Lord, you kill and you make alive.
  You bring down to Sheol and you raise up.
You make poor and make rich.
  You bring low and you lift up.
You raise the poor out of the dust.
  You lift up the needy from the dunghill
  to make them sit with princes
  and inherit the throne of glory.
For the pillars of the earth are yours, Lord.
  You have set the world on them.
You will guard the feet of your holy ones,
  but the wicked will be put to silence in darkness;
  for no man will prevail by strength.
Those who strive with you will be broken to pieces.
  You will thunder against them in the sky.
You will judge the ends of the earth.
  You will give me strength,
  and exalt the horn of your anointed.

I praise you, Lord!

JOSHUA 4:23-24; JUDGES 5:2-5; 1 SAMUEL 2:6-10; JOB 12:10

PSALMS

Lord, you are my shepherd;
    I will lack nothing.
You make me lie down in green pastures.
    You lead me beside still waters.
    You restore my soul.
You guide me in the paths of righteousness for your
        name's sake.
Even though I walk through the valley of the shadow
        of death,
    I will fear no evil, for you are with me.
Your rod and your staff,
    they comfort me.
You prepare a table before me
    in the presence of my enemies.
You anoint my head with oil.
    My cup runs over.
Surely goodness and lovingkindness shall follow me all
        the days of my life,
    and I will dwell in your house, Lord, forever.

To you, Lord, I lift up my soul.
    My God, I have trusted in you.
    No one who waits for you will be shamed.
You are the God of my salvation;
    your tender mercies and your lovingkindness are from
        of old.
Good and upright are you.
    You guide the humble in justice.
You teach the humble your way.
    All your paths, Lord, are lovingkindness and truth.
For your name's sake, Lord,
    you have pardoned my iniquity.
Your friendship is with me, Lord.
    You have shown me your covenant.
My eyes are ever on you.

PSALM 23:1-6; 25:1-3, 5-6, 8-11, 14-15

THE LOVING AND FAITHFUL GOD

For your word's sake, Lord, and according to your own heart, you work greatness. O Lord, you are great. There is no one like you, neither is there any God besides you.

You have redeemed for yourself a people, and made yourself a name, and done great things for us. You established us for yourself to be your people forever; and you became our God.

Lord, you save the humble,
　　but your eyes are on the arrogant,
　　that you may bring them down.
For you are my lamp, O Lord;
　　my God who lightens my darkness.
By you, I can run against a troop.
　　By my God, I can leap over a wall.
God, your way is perfect.
　　Your word proves to be true.
　　You are a shield to all those who take refuge in you.
For who is God, besides you, Lord?
　　Who is a rock, besides my God?
You are my strong fortress.
　　You make my way perfect.
You make my feet like hinds' feet,
　　and set me on my high places.
You teach my hands to war,
　　so that my arms bend a bow of bronze.
You have also given me the shield of your salvation.
　　Your gentleness has made me great.
You have enlarged my steps under me.
　　My feet have not slipped.

I praise you, Lord!

2 SAMUEL 7:21-24; 22:28-37

FATHER, SON, SPIRIT

Holy Spirit, you are the Spirit of God, the Spirit of the Father, the Spirit of Christ. You are the Lord.

You are the Spirit of life.
The Spirit of truth.
The Spirit of power.
The Spirit of love.
The Spirit of holiness.
The Spirit of comfort.
The Spirit of joy.
The Spirit of glory.
The Spirit of grace.

You proceed from the Father. You are the Counselor whom the Father sends in Jesus's name.

Holy Spirit, thank you that when I trusted in the name of Jesus for the forgiveness of my sins, I received you as a gift. That promise from God is for me, and for my children, and for all who are far off—everyone the Lord my God will call to himself.

It's the Father who has given you to me. You are with me forever. You've been poured out on me richly through Jesus Christ my Savior. He gave you to me without measure.

Now, you live in me. I am your temple—a holy temple.

You have birthed me. That which is born of the flesh is flesh. That which is born of you is spirit. I am born of you. Through you I have entered into God's kingdom.

Holy Spirit, you are the Spirit of adoption. I didn't receive a spirit of slavery that produces fear. I received you.

By you I cry out to God, "Abba! Father!"

You testify along with my own spirit that I am God's child. I am his heir, a joint heir with Christ.

Holy Spirit, I praise you!

JOHN 3:5-6, 33-35; 14:16-18, 26; 15:26; ACTS 1:8; 2:38-39; 9:31; ROMANS 1:4; 8:2, 15-17; 15:30; 1 CORINTHIANS 3:16; 6:19; 1 THESSALONIANS 1:6; 4:8; 2 TIMOTHY 1:4; TITUS 3:6; HEBREWS 10:29; 1 PETER 4:12

CHRIST'S VICTORY

Jesus, you were led as a sheep to the slaughter.
    As a lamb before his shearer is silent,
    so you didn't open your mouth.
In your humiliation, justice was denied you.
    For your life was taken from the earth.

You suffered for me. You didn't sin, neither was deceit
found in your mouth. When you were cursed, you didn't
curse back. When you suffered, you didn't threaten, but
committed yourself to him who judges righteously.

You yourself bore my sins in your body on the tree. I am
healed by your wounds.

At the sixth hour that day, darkness came over the whole
land until the ninth hour. The sun was darkened.

You cried with a loud voice, and said, "It is finished."
Then you bowed your head, and gave up your spirit.

The veil of the temple was torn in two from the top to
the bottom.

Jesus, you were delivered up by the determined counsel
and foreknowledge of God.

By lawless men you were crucified and killed; but God raised
you up, freeing you from the agony of death, because it
wasn't possible that you should be held by it.

At the tomb, two men in dazzling clothing said to the women,
"Why do you seek the living among the dead? He is not here,
but he has risen."

Just as you said: you had to be delivered up into the hands
of sinful men and be crucified, and the third day rise again.

Jesus, you were declared with power to be the Son of God
by your resurrection from the dead.

I praise you!

MATTHEW 27:50-51; LUKE 23:44-45; 24:1-7, 26; JOHN 19:30; ACTS 2:23-24;
8:32-33; ROMANS 1:4; 1 PETER 2:21-23

PSALMS

Lord, your lovingkindness is before my eyes.
I make my voice of thanksgiving heard
    and tell of all your wondrous deeds.
I love the place where your glory dwells.
    I bless you, Lord.

I will bless you, Lord, at all times.
    Your praise will always be in my mouth.
    My soul will boast in you.
Magnify the Lord with me.
    Let's exalt his name together.
Lord, you deliver me from all my fears.
    I look to you, and I am radiant.
    My face will never be covered with shame.
I cried and you heard me,
    and saved me out of all my troubles.
Your angel encamps around those who fear you;
    you deliver me.
Oh, taste and see that the Lord is good!
    Blessed is the man who takes refuge in you.
Oh, fear the Lord, you his saints,
    for there is no lack with those who fear him.
The young lions do lack, and suffer hunger,
    but those who seek you, Lord, shall not lack any
        good thing.
The righteous cry, and you hear, Lord,
    and deliver them out of all their troubles.
You are near to those who have a broken heart,
    and save those who have a crushed spirit.
Many are the afflictions of the righteous,
    but you deliver him out of them all.
Lord, you redeem the soul of your servants.
    None who take refuge in you will be condemned.

I praise you, Lord!

PSALM 26:3, 7-8, 12; 34:1-10, 17-19, 22

THINGS TO COME

Jesus, you are the righteous Branch that God raised up to David.
You will reign as king and deal wisely,
  and will execute justice and righteousness in the land.
In your days Judah will be saved,
  and Israel will dwell safely.
This is your name by which you will be called:
  The Lord our Righteousness.

You will show wonders in the heavens and in the earth:
  blood, fire, and pillars of smoke.
The sun will be turned into darkness,
  and the moon into blood,
  before the great and terrible day of the Lord comes.
It will happen that whoever will call on your name,
    Lord, will be saved.
In Mount Zion and in Jerusalem there will be those
    who escape,
  just as you promised.
The remnant will be those whom you call.

I sing and rejoice, Lord, for you will come and dwell with
your people.

Many nations will join themselves to you in that day and
will be your people; and you will dwell among us.

Jesus, we will know that the Lord of hosts has sent you to us.

Lord, you will inherit Judah as your portion in the holy
land, and will again choose Jerusalem.

All flesh will be silent before you.

You will be King over all the earth. In that day you will be
one, and your name will be one.

I praise you, Lord!

JEREMIAH 23:5-6; JOEL 2:30-32; ZECHARIAH 2:10-13; 14:9

6TH SEVEN PRAISES

*... giving thanks always
and for everything to God the Father
in the name of our Lord Jesus Christ ...*
Ephesians 5:20, ESV

The Sovereign Creator of All

Lord, you are the God of glory. You are righteous. You are enthroned above the cherubim.

You alone are God of all the kingdoms of the earth. You made heaven and earth. I bless you!

You are greater than all gods. Who is able to build you a house, since heaven, even highest heaven, cannot contain you? Will you indeed dwell with men on the earth, God? If heaven and the heaven of heavens can't contain you; how much less a house built with hands!

Lord, you are God in heaven. You are ruler over all the kingdoms of the nations. Power and might are in your hand, so that none is able to withstand you.

You are blessed, Lord, forever and ever. Yours is the greatness, the power, the glory, the victory, and the majesty! For all that is in the heavens and in the earth is yours.

Yours is the kingdom, Lord, and you are exalted as head above all.

Both riches and honor come from you, and you rule over all. In your hand are power and might. It is in your hand to make great, and to give strength to all.

Therefore, I thank you, God, and praise your glorious name.

I bless you from everlasting to everlasting! Blessed be your glorious name, which is exalted above all blessing and praise. You are the Lord—you alone.

You have made heaven, the heaven of heavens, with all their army, the earth and all that is on it, the seas and all that is in them, and you preserve them all. The host of heaven worships you.

I worship you, Lord!

1 Samuel 2:5-6; 6:8; 15:28-29; 20:6; 1 Kings 8:27; 2 Kings 19:15; 1 Chronicles 29:10-13; 2 Chronicles 2:12; Ezra 9:15; Nehemiah 9:5-6

PSALMS

Lord, you are my rock.
> Blessed be you!

You are my strength and my shield.
> My heart trusts in you, and I am helped.

Therefore my heart greatly rejoices.
> With my song I will thank you.

You are my strength.
> You are a stronghold of salvation to me.

You are my shepherd;
> you bear me up forever.

I ascribe to you, Lord.
> I ascribe to you glory and strength.

I ascribe to you the glory due your name.
> I worship you in holiness.

Your voice is on the waters, Lord.
> The God of glory thunders, even you, Lord, on many
> waters.

Your voice is powerful.
> Your voice is full of majesty.

> Your voice breaks in pieces the cedars of Lebanon.

Your voice strikes with flashes of lightning.
> Your voice shakes the wilderness.

> You shake the wilderness of Kadesh.

Your voice makes the deer calve,
> and strips the forests bare.

> In your temple everything says, "Glory!"

Lord, you sat enthroned at the Flood.
> Yes, you sit as King forever.

You give strength to your people.
> You bless your people with peace.

Lord, you have made my days like the width of my hand.
> My lifetime is as nothing before you.

Surely every man stands as a breath.
> But my hope is in you.

PSALM 28:6-9; 29:1-11; 39:5, 7

THE LOVING AND FAITHFUL GOD

Lord, you are my rock, my fortress,
　　and my deliverer, even mine.
You are my rock in whom I take refuge;
　　my shield, and the horn of my salvation,
　　my high tower, my refuge, my savior.
I call on you, who are worthy to be praised;
　　so shall I be saved from my enemies.
For the waves of death surrounded me.
　　The floods of ungodliness made me afraid.
In my distress, I called on you, Lord.
　　Yes, I called to you, my God.
You heard my voice; my cry came to your ears.
　　Then the earth shook and trembled.
The foundations of heaven quaked and were shaken,
　　because you were angry.
Smoke went up out of your nostrils.
　　Consuming fire came out of your mouth.
You bowed the heavens and came down.
　　Thick darkness was under your feet.
You made darkness a shelter around yourself:
　　gathering of waters, and thick clouds of the skies.
At the brightness before you, coals of fire were kindled.
　　You thundered from heaven;
　　you, the Most High, uttered your voice.
　　You sent out lightning and scattered and confused them.
Then the channels of the sea appeared.
　　The foundations of the world were laid bare by your
　　　　rebuke,
　　at the blast of the breath of your nostrils.
Lord, you sent from on high and took me.
　　You drew me out of many waters.
You delivered me from my strong enemy,
　　from those who hated me, for they were too mighty for me.
They came on me in the day of my calamity,
　　but you were my support.
You brought me out into a large place.
　　You delivered me, because you delighted in me.

2 SAMUEL 22:2-20

FATHER, SON, SPIRIT

Father, you are true. You give the Spirit without measure. You love the Son, and you have given all things into his hand.

You are spirit. I worship you in spirit and in truth.

You have life in yourself, and you gave to the Son also to have life in himself.

You didn't send your Son into the world to judge the world, but that the world should be saved through him.

You sent the Son to be the Savior of the world. You who sent Jesus are true. You are the One who glorifies Jesus.

You glorified the Son, that the Son might glorify you. You gave Jesus authority over all people, so he would give eternal life to all you gave him. You gave me to Jesus, for I am yours.

Father, you sanctify me in your truth. Your word is truth.

Righteous Father, the world hasn't known you, but I know you, because I know that you sent Jesus.

By your grace I could turn from darkness to light, from the power of Satan to you. So my sins were forgiven and I received an inheritance in Jesus.

Through him you reconciled me to yourself. I rejoice in you!

Father, your wisdom is not of this world, nor of the rulers of this world who are coming to nothing.

Your wisdom is in a mystery. It has been hidden. You fore-ordained it before the worlds for my glory.

Christ is your mystery, and your wisdom. The preaching of his cross is your power toward me.

Father, I glorify you!

JOHN 3:17, 33-35; 4:14, 24; 5:26; 8:26, 54; 17:1-2, 9, 17, 25; ACTS 11:18; 26:18; ROMANS 5:11; 1 CORINTHIANS 1:18, 24; 2:6-7; 2 CORINTHIANS 5:18; COLOSSIANS 2:2-3

CHRIST'S VICTORY

Jesus, you are God revealed in the flesh,
    vindicated by the Spirit,
    seen by angels,
    preached among the nations,
    believed on in the world,
    and received up in glory.

David prophesied about your resurrection, that your soul
wouldn't be left in Hades, nor would your flesh see decay.
But God glorified you, raising you from the dead, and you
were exalted to the right hand of God.

You descended into the lower parts of the earth. You who
descended are the one who ascended far above all the
heavens, that you might fill all things.

You died for our sins according to the Scriptures, you were
buried, and you were raised on the third day according to
the Scriptures.

You were received up into heaven and you sat down at the
right hand of God.

You received from the Father the promise of the Holy Spirit
and poured him out upon all flesh.

God appointed you as the Judge of the living and the dead.
All the prophets testify about you, that through your name
everyone who believes in you will receive forgiveness of sins.

Jesus, you are the holy and righteous one. You are the Prince
of life, the one God raised from the dead. Through you my
sins are blotted out.

You are the fulfillment of what the Father promised to
Abraham, "All the families of the earth will be blessed
through your offspring."

Jesus, I praise you!

MARK 16:19; ACTS 2:30-33; 3:13-15, 19, 25; 10:38; 1 CORINTHIANS 15:3-4;
EPHESIANS 4:9-10; 1 TIMOTHY 3:16

PSALMS

I will extol you, Lord,
for you have raised me up.
Sing praise to him, you saints of his.
Give thanks to his holy name.
Your favor, Lord, is for a lifetime.
You have turned my mourning into dancing for me.
You clothed me with gladness,
so that my heart may sing praise to you, and not be silent.
O Lord my God, I will give thanks to you forever!

In you, Lord, I take refuge.
You are my rock and my fortress;
you are my stronghold.
Into your hand I commend my spirit.
You redeem me, Lord, God of truth.
I will be glad and rejoice in your lovingkindness.
You have not shut me up into the hand of the enemy.
You have set my feet in a large place.
I trust in you, Lord.
I said, "You are my God."
My times are in your hand.
Oh, how great is your goodness,
which you have laid up for those who fear you,
which you have worked for those who take refuge in you,
before the sons of men!
In the shelter of your presence you will hide me from the
plotting of man.
You will keep me secretly in a dwelling,
away from the strife of tongues.
Praise be to you, Lord,
for you have shown me your marvelous lovingkindness.
Oh, love the Lord, all you his saints!
You, Lord, preserve the faithful.
My hope is in you.

PSALM 30:1, 4-5, 11-12; 31:1, 3-5, 7-8, 14-15, 19-21, 23-24

THINGS TO COME

Lord, you decreed seventy sets of seven years for your people and for your holy city.

These sets would finish transgression, put an end to sin, make atonement for iniquity, and bring in everlasting righteousness.

I praise you! Vision and prophecy would be sealed up, and the most holy place anointed.

Jesus, from the command to restore and rebuild Jerusalem, until you, the Anointed One, would be seven sets of seven and sixty-two sets of seven.

After the sixty-two sets of seven, you, the Anointed One, would be killed and have nothing.

The people of the prince to come would destroy the city and the sanctuary. Its end would come with a flood. From then until the end, war and desolations were decreed.

The prince would make a firm covenant with many for one set of seven. In the middle of it, he would cause sacrifices and offerings to cease.

On the wing of abominations would come one who makes things desolate, until the end decreed for him comes, and wrath is poured out on him.

Then Michael will stand up, the great prince who stands for the children of your people, Lord. There will be a time of trouble, unlike any since there was a nation.

That's when your people will be delivered, everyone who is found written in the book. Many of those who sleep in the dust of the earth will awake, some to everlasting life, and some to shame and everlasting contempt.

Those who are wise will shine as the brightness of the expanse. Those who turn many to righteousness will shine as the stars forever and ever.

I praise you, Lord!

DANIEL 9:24-27; 12:1-3

7TH SEVEN PRAISES

Yet you are holy,
O You who are enthroned
upon the praises of Israel.
PSALM 22:3, NASB

THE SOVEREIGN CREATOR OF ALL

Sing to the Lord, all the earth!
    Display his salvation from day to day.
Declare his glory among the nations,
    and his marvelous works among all the peoples.
For you are great, Lord, and greatly to be praised.
    You are to be feared above all gods.
All the gods of the peoples are idols,
    but you made the heavens.
Splendor and majesty are before you.
    Strength and gladness are in your place.
Ascribe to the Lord, O families of the peoples,
    ascribe to the Lord glory and strength!
Ascribe to the Lord the glory due to his name.
    Come before him and worship in holy array.
Tremble before him, all the earth.
    The world is established; it can't be moved.
Let the heavens be glad,
    and let the earth rejoice!
    Let them say among the nations, "The Lord reigns!"
Let the sea roar, and its fullness!
    Let the field exult, and all that is in it!
Then the trees of the forest will sing for joy before you, Lord,
    for you come to judge the earth.

Your hands have framed me and fashioned me, Lord.
    You have fashioned me as clay.
You have clothed me with skin and flesh,
    and knit me together with bones and sinews.
    You have granted me life and lovingkindness.
I give thanks to you, Lord, for you are good;
    your lovingkindness endures forever.
You are the God of my salvation!
    I give thanks to your holy name,
    and glory in your praise.
Blessed be you, O God,
    from everlasting to everlasting.

1 CHRONICLES 16:23-36; JOB 10:8-12

Psalms

I am blessed, Lord. You have forgiven my disobedience and
  covered my sin.
I am blessed, Lord, for you have not imputed my iniquity
  to me.
Lord, you are my hiding place.
  You preserve me from trouble.
  You surround me with songs of deliverance.
You instruct me and teach me in the way which I should go.
  You counsel me with your eye on me.
  Your lovingkindness, Lord, surrounds me, for I trust in you.
Be glad in the Lord, and rejoice, you righteous!
  Shout for joy, all you who are upright in heart!

My soul will be joyful in you, Lord.
  I will rejoice in your salvation.
Who, Lord, is like you,
  who delivers the poor from him who is too strong for him;
  yes, the poor and the needy from him who robs him?
I will give you thanks in the great assembly.
  I will praise you among many people.
All day long my tongue will speak of your righteousness and
  your praise.

Your lovingkindness, Lord, is in the heavens.
  Your faithfulness reaches to the skies.
Your righteousness is like the mountains of God.
  Your judgments are like a great deep.
  Lord, you preserve man and animal.
How precious is your lovingkindness, God!
  The children of men take refuge under the shadow of
  your wings.
I will feast in the abundance of your house.
  You will make me drink of the river of your pleasures.
For with you is the spring of life.
  In your light I see light.
Your lovingkindness is toward those who know you;
  your righteousness, Lord, is toward me.

Psalm 32:1-2, 7-8, 11; 35:9-10, 18, 28; 36:5-10

THE LOVING AND FAITHFUL GOD

Lord, you live!
  Blessed be my rock!
Exalted be you, God, the rock of my salvation.
  You execute vengeance for me.
  You bring me out from my enemies.
You lift me up above those who rise up against me.
  You deliver me from the violent man.
I will give thanks to you, God, among the nations,
  and will sing praises to your name.
You give great deliverance to me,
  and show lovingkindness to me forevermore.

O Lord, there is no God like you, in heaven above or on
earth beneath.

I give thanks to you, Lord.
  I call on your name.
  I make known what you have done among the peoples.
I sing to you.
  I sing praises to you
  and tell of all your marvelous works.
I glory in your holy name.
  Let the hearts of those who seek you rejoice.
I seek you and your strength and
  your face forevermore.
I remember the marvelous works you have done,
  your wonders, and the judgments of your mouth.
You are the Lord my God.
  Your judgments are in all the earth.
You commanded your covenant for a thousand generations.

I give you thanks, Lord, because your lovingkindness
endures forever. You keep covenant and lovingkindness with
your servants; you fulfill your promises. You spoke with your
mouth and have fulfilled it with your hand.

I praise you!

2 SAMUEL 22:47-51; 1 KINGS 8:23; 1 CHRONICLES 16:8-15, 41;
2 CHRONICLES 6:14-15

FATHER, SON, SPIRIT

Jesus, you were conceived of the Holy Spirit. You were named Jesus, for you came to save your people from their sins.

You are Father's beloved Son. He is well pleased with you. On you the Spirit descended as a dove.

You baptize in the Holy Spirit, and with fire.

When you appeared, the people who sat in darkness saw a great light; to those who sat in the region of the shadow of death, light dawned.

Jesus, you give rest to all who labor and are heavily burdened. You are gentle and humble in heart. I take your yoke upon me and learn from you, and I find rest for my soul. Your yoke is easy, and your burden is light.

You are the Son of Man, the Son of the living God, the Christ. You are my Master.

You came to seek and save that which was lost.

The Father said to you, "Sit on my right hand, until I make your enemies a footstool for your feet."

When you took Peter and James and John up on the mountain, you were changed before them. They saw your glory. Your face shone like the sun, and your garments became as white as light.

Jesus, you went about all the cities and villages, teaching and preaching the good news of the kingdom, and healing every disease and every sickness among the people. You had compassion on them.

When people saw the mute speaking, the injured healed, the lame walking, and the blind seeing, they glorified the God of Israel.

All authority has been given to you in heaven and on earth, Jesus. You are with me always, even to the end of the age. I praise you!

MATTHEW 1:20; 3:11, 16-17; 4:16; 9:35-36; 11:28-30; 12:7; 14:14; 15:31; 16:16; 17:1-2; 18:11; 22:44; 23:10; 28:16, 20; LUKE 19:10

CHRIST'S VICTORY

Jesus, you are the eternal life. You are the true God and eternal life.

Father, you so loved the world, that you gave your one and only Son, that whoever believes in him should not perish, but have eternal life.

This is your will: that everyone who sees the Son, and believes in him, should have eternal life. Jesus himself will raise us up on the last day.

You gave me eternal life, Father. This life is in your Son. I who have the Son have the life.

Father, the wages of sin is death, but your free gift is eternal life through Christ Jesus my Lord.

Eternal life is this: that I know you, Father, the only true God, and Jesus Christ whom you sent.

Jesus, you laid down your life for me. Whoever hears your word and believes the One who sent you has eternal life. Because of you, I will not come into judgment, but I have passed out of death into life.

The Father set his seal on you. You are the living bread which came down out of heaven, that anyone may eat of it and not die. If anyone eats of this bread, he will live forever.

Jesus, the Father gave you authority over all people, so you would give eternal life to all he gave you.

Whoever believes in you, Jesus, has eternal life. I know I have eternal life.

I praise you!

JOHN 3:16, 36; 5:21, 24; 6:27, 40, 50-51; 17:2-3; ROMANS 6:23; 1 JOHN 3:16; 5:11-12, 20

PSALMS

Rejoice in the Lord, you righteous!
 Praise is fitting for the upright.
Give thanks to the Lord with the lyre.
 Sing praises to him with the harp.
I sing to you a new song, Lord.
 I play skillfully with a shout of joy!
For your word is right.
 All your work is done in faithfulness.
You love righteousness and justice.
 The earth is full of your lovingkindness.
By your word, the heavens were made:
 all their army by the breath of your mouth.
You gather the waters of the sea together as a heap.
 You lay up the deeps in storehouses.
Let all the earth fear you, Lord.
 Let all the inhabitants of the world stand in awe of you.
For you spoke, and it was done.
 You commanded, and it stood firm.
You bring the counsel of the nations to nothing.
 You make the thoughts of the peoples to be of no effect.
Your counsel, Lord, stands fast forever,
 the thoughts of your heart to all generations.
Blessed are the people you have chosen
 for your own inheritance.
You look from heaven and see all the sons of men,
 you who fashion their hearts, and consider all of their works.
No king is saved by the multitude of an army.
 A mighty man is not delivered by great strength.
Lord, your eye is on those who fear you,
 on those who hope in your lovingkindness.
My soul has waited for you, Lord.
 You are my help and my shield.
My heart rejoices in you,
 because I have trusted in your holy name.
Your lovingkindness is on me, Lord,
 since I have hoped in you.

PSALM 33:1-16, 18, 20-22

THINGS TO COME

Jesus, at the end of this age, you will send out your angels, and they will gather out of your kingdom all things that cause stumbling and those who do iniquity, and will cast them into the furnace of fire.

Then the righteous will shine like the sun in the kingdom of their Father.

You are the Son of Man. You will come in the glory of your Father with your angels, and then you will render to everyone according to his deeds.

Jesus, the sun will be darkened, the moon will not give its light, the stars will fall from the sky, and the powers of the heavens will be shaken; and then the sign of you, the Son of Man, will appear in the sky.

All the tribes of the earth will mourn, and they will see you coming on the clouds of the sky with power and great glory.

You will send out your angels with a great sound of a trumpet, and they will gather together your chosen ones from the four winds, from one end of the sky to the other.

When you, the Son of Man, come in your glory, and all the holy angels with you, then you will sit on the throne of your glory.

Before you all the nations will be gathered, and you will separate them one from another, as a shepherd separates the sheep from the goats.

You will set the sheep on your right hand, but the goats on the left. These will go away into eternal punishment, but the righteous into eternal life.

Jesus, I praise you!

MATTHEW 13:41-43; 16:27; 24:29-31; 25:31-33, 46

8TH SEVEN PRAISES

Praise the Lord!
For it is good to sing praises to our God;
for it is pleasant and fitting to praise him.
Sing to the Lord with thanksgiving;
sing praises on the harp to our God!
Praise the Lord!

Psalm 147:1, 7, 20

The Sovereign Creator of All

Lord, you do great things that can't be fathomed,
    marvelous things without number.
You give rain on the earth,
    and send waters on the fields.
You set on high those who are low;
    those who mourn are lifted to safety.
You catch the wise in their own craftiness;
    and bring to an end the schemes of the cunning.
You save from the sword of their mouth,
    even the needy from the hand of the mighty.
So the poor have hope,
    and injustice shuts her mouth.

God, you are wise in heart and mighty in strength.
    You remove mountains, and they don't know it,
    when you overturn them in your anger.
You shake the earth out of its place.
    Its pillars tremble.
You command the sun and it doesn't rise;
    you seal up the stars.
You alone stretch out the heavens,
    and tread on the waves of the sea.
You made the Bear, Orion, and the Pleiades,
    and the chambers of the south.
You do great things past finding out;
    yes, marvelous things without number.

With you is awesome majesty.
    You are exalted in power.
In justice and great righteousness, you will not oppress.
    I revere you, Lord.

Job 5:9-16; 9:4-10; 37:22-24

Psalms

Lord, I delight myself in you,
    and you give me the desires of my heart.
I commit my way to you.
    I trust also in you, and you will do it.
You will make my righteousness shine out like light,
    and my justice as the noonday sun.
I rest in you, Lord, and wait patiently for you.
    You uphold the righteous.
You know the days of the blameless.
    My inheritance will be forever.
My steps are established by you, Lord.
    You delight in my way.
Though I stumble, I will not fall,
    for you hold me up with your hand.
Lord, you love justice,
    and you don't forsake your saints.
    You preserve us forever.
The salvation of the righteous is from you.
    You are my stronghold in the time of trouble.
You help me and rescue me,
    because I have taken refuge in you.

As the deer pants for the water brooks,
    so my soul pants after you, God.
My soul thirsts for you, for the living God.
    I hope in you, God!
    I will still praise you for the saving help of your presence.
Deep calls to deep at the sound of your waterfalls.
    All your waves and your billows have swept over me.
You command your lovingkindness in the daytime.
    In the night your song will be with me:
    a prayer to the God of my life.
I hope in you, God! I will praise you,
    the saving help of my countenance, and my God.

Psalm 37:4-7, 18, 23-24, 28, 39-40; 42:1-2, 5, 7-8, 11

THE LOVING AND FAITHFUL GOD

Father, you built David a house. You established his throne forever.

According to your own heart, God, you have done all this greatness, to make known all these great things. There is no one like you, Lord, neither is there any God besides you. Let your name be established and magnified forever.

Lord, you love your people. You are good; your lovingkindness endures forever.

I worship you and give you thanks. You are good; your lovingkindness endures forever.

You are the God of heaven, the great and awesome God, who keeps covenant and lovingkindness with those who love you. You redeemed me by your great power and by your strong hand.

You are the Lord, the God who chose Abram, brought him out of Ur of the Chaldees, gave him the name of Abraham, and found his heart faithful before you. You made a covenant with him, to give to his offspring the land of the Canaanite. You kept your promise, Lord, for you are righteous.

You are my God, the great, the mighty, and the awesome God, who keeps covenant and lovingkindness.

I know that my Redeemer lives.
    In the end, you will take your stand upon the earth.
I will see you in my flesh, God.
I myself will behold you on my side.
    My own eyes will see this, not those of a stranger.

Lord, I praise you!

1 CHRONICLES 17:13-14, 19-20, 24; 2 CHRONICLES 2:12; 5:13; 7:3;
NEHEMIAH 1:5, 10; 9:7-8, 32; JOB 19:25-27

FATHER, SON, SPIRIT

Eternal Spirit, you are the Spirit of my Father.

You raised up Jesus from the dead, and through you he offered himself without blemish to God.

Jesus sent you, the promise of the Father, upon the disciples. They were clothed with power from on high. On the day of Pentecost, all the disciples were filled with you. They began to speak with other tongues, as you gave them utterance.

Holy Spirit, you are one God has given to me.

You are the one who has sanctified me.

Spirit of the Living God, you are the one who gives life. The flesh profits nothing.

Those living in the flesh can't please God, but I am no longer in the flesh. I am in you, Holy Spirit. You dwell in me.

As I set my mind on you, I have life and peace.

You set me free from the law of sin and death.

I am a letter of Christ, written by you on the tablet of my heart.

I don't serve God in the old way of the written law. God released me from that. You are the new way. You make me sufficient as a servant of a new covenant.

Spirit, you help me in my weakness. I don't know how to pray as I should, but you intercede for me according to God's will with groanings which can't be uttered.

Holy Spirit, I praise you! I am a child of the Father. I am led by you.

God's kingdom is righteousness, peace, and joy in you.

MATTHEW 10:19; LUKE 10:21; 24:49; JOHN 6:63; ACTS 2:1, 4; 4:32; ROMANS 7:4-6; 8:2, 6, 8-9, 11, 14, 26-27; 14:17; 15:16; 2 CORINTHIANS 3:3-5; HEBREWS 9:14

CHRIST'S VICTORY

Father, I am not saved by my own works, but by your grace through faith. It is not of me; it is a gift from you.

I praise you that by grace I have been saved. And if I was saved by grace, then it couldn't be by my works; otherwise grace is no longer grace.

Father, by your grace I am made right with you by faith. It has nothing to do with the works of the law.

You have justified me freely by your grace through the redemption that is in Christ Jesus. You sent him to be my atoning sacrifice, through faith in his blood.

Abraham believed you, and you counted it to him for righteousness. I have believed you as well. So I am a child of Abraham.

You have made me right with you by faith, just as you did Abraham.

You spoke your promises to Abraham and to his offspring, Christ. I praise you that the inheritance was never based on the law, because you gave it to Abraham by a promise.

Jesus, you redeemed me from the curse of the law. You became a curse for me. You were hung on a tree, so that the blessing of Abraham might come to me, that I might receive the promise of the Spirit simply by believing.

Father, because you have justified me by faith, I have peace with you through my Lord Jesus. I stand in grace. I rejoice in hope of your glory.

By your grace you have made me an heir of the world with Abraham. Your promise to me is sure.

All praise to you, Father!

Romans 3:22-27; 4:16; 5:1-2; 11:6; Galatians 2:16; 3:6-9, 13-14, 17-18; Ephesians 2:5, 8-9; Philippians 3:9

PSALMS

Lord, you delight in me;
　　you set me in your presence forever.
I will bless you, Lord God,
　　from everlasting to everlasting!

I waited patiently for you, Lord.
　　You turned to me, and heard my cry.
You brought me up out of a horrible pit,
　　out of the miry clay.
You set my feet on a rock,
　　and gave me a firm place to stand.
You have put a new song in my mouth, even praise to
　　　my God.
　　Many will see it, and fear, and will trust in you.
　　Blessed is the man who makes you his trust.
O Lord my God, many are the wonderful works you
　　　have done,
　　and your thoughts which are toward me.
I can't declare them all back to you.
　　They are more than can be counted.
I delight to do your will, my God.
　　Yes, your law is within my heart.
I have proclaimed glad news of righteousness in the great
　　　assembly.
　　I will not seal my lips, Lord.
I haven't hidden your righteousness.
　　I have declared your faithfulness and your salvation.
I haven't concealed your lovingkindness and your truth
　　　from the great assembly.
　　Your lovingkindness and your truth continually
　　　preserve me.
All who seek you will rejoice and be glad in you.
　　Those who love your salvation will continually say,
　　"Let the Lord be exalted!"

I exalt you, Lord!

PSALM 40:1-5, 8-11, 16; 41:11-13

THINGS TO COME

Jesus, we will see you, the Son of Man, sitting at the right hand of Power, and coming on the clouds of the sky.

You will come back in the glory of your Father with your holy angels.

In those days, the sun will be darkened, the moon will not give its light, the stars will fall from the sky, and the powers that are in the heavens will be shaken.

Then we will see you coming in clouds with great power and glory.

You will send out your angels, and will gather together your chosen ones from the four winds, from the ends of the earth to the ends of the sky.

You are coming at an hour when we don't expect you. As the lightning flashes out of one part of the sky and shines to another part, so will you be in your day.

Thank you that those who are considered worthy to attain to the coming age and the resurrection from the dead can't die anymore, for they are like the angels, and are children of God, being children of the resurrection.

Jesus, you are the Christ, the Son of the Blessed One. I will see you sitting at the right hand of Power, and coming with the clouds of the sky.

You are the Son of Man. You will come in your glory, and the glory of the Father, and of the holy angels.

I praise you, Jesus!

MATTHEW 26:64; MARK 8:38; 13:24-27; 14:61-62; LUKE 9:26; 12:40; 17:24; 20:35-36

9TH SEVEN PRAISES

But you are a chosen people,
a royal priesthood, a holy nation,
God's special possession, that you may
declare the praises of him who called you
out of darkness into his wonderful light.

1 PETER 2:9, NIV

THE SOVEREIGN CREATOR OF ALL

God, can I fathom your mysteries?
  Can I probe the limits of the Almighty?
They are high as heaven.
  They are deeper than Sheol.
Their measure is longer than the earth,
  and broader than the sea.

God, with you is wisdom and might.
  You have counsel and understanding.
If you tear down, it can't be built again.
  If you shut a man in, no one can release.
If you withhold the waters, they dry up.
  If you send them out, they overrun the earth.
With you is strength and wisdom.
  The deceived and the deceiver are yours.
You lead counselors away stripped.
  You make judges fools.
You loosen the bond of kings.
  You bind their waist with a belt.
You overthrow the mighty.
  You remove the speech of those who are trusted.
You pour contempt on princes,
  and loosen the belt of the strong.
You uncover deep things out of darkness,
  and bring into the light the shadow of death.
You make nations great and you destroy them.
  You enlarge the nations and lead them captive.
You take away understanding from the chiefs of the people
      of the earth;
  they grope in the dark without light.

Dominion and awe are with you, God.
  You make peace in your high places.
Can your armies be counted?
  On whom does your light not arise?
I praise you, Lord!

JOB 11:7-9; 12:13-25; 25:2-3

PSALMS

Lord, you are the God of my strength.
You send out your light and your truth.
> They lead me to you.

I come to you, to God, my exceeding joy.
> I will praise you, God, my God.
I hope in you, God!
> I will praise you:
> my Savior, my helper, and my God.

God, you are my King.
> Through your name, I tread down those who rise up
> > against me.
You have saved me from my adversaries;
> in you I make my boast all day long.
> I will give thanks to your name forever.
You have redeemed me for your lovingkindness' sake.

Your throne, God, is forever and ever.
> A scepter of equity is the scepter of your kingdom.
You have loved righteousness, and hated wickedness.
> Therefore God, your God, has anointed you with the oil
> > of gladness above your companions.
I will make your name to be remembered in all generations.
> The peoples will give you thanks forever and ever.

Great are you, Lord, and greatly to be praised,
> in the city of my God, in your holy mountain.
You are the great King.
> You are the God of hosts.
You will establish your city forever.
> I meditate on your lovingkindness, God.
As is your name,
> so is your praise to the ends of the earth.
> Your right hand is full of righteousness.
You are my God forever and ever.
> You will be my guide even to death.

Psalm 43:2-5; 44:4-5, 7-8, 26; 45:6-7, 17; 48:1-2, 8-10, 14

THE LOVING AND FAITHFUL GOD

Lord, though my sins were as scarlet, they are as white as snow.
Though they were red like crimson, they are as wool.

Lord, you yourself gave us a sign. The virgin conceived, and
bore a son, and called his name Immanuel.

The people who walked in darkness saw a great light.
The light shined on those who lived in the land of the
     shadow of death.

Jesus, you are the child born to us, the son given to us. The
government will be on your shoulders. Your name is called

> Wonderful Counselor,
> Mighty God,
> Everlasting Father,
> Prince of Peace.

Of the increase of your government and of peace there
shall be no end. You will be on David's throne and over his
kingdom, to establish it and to uphold it with justice and
with righteousness forever. The zeal of God, the Lord of
hosts, will perform this.

I will give thanks to you, O Lord;
     you comfort me.
You are my salvation;
     I will trust, and will not be afraid;
For you, Lord God, are my strength and my song;
     you have become my salvation.
     I draw water from the wells of your salvation.
I give thanks to you,
     I call upon your name,
I make known your deeds among the peoples,
     and proclaim that your name is exalted.
I sing praise to you, Lord, for you have done gloriously;
     let this be made known in all the earth.
I shout and sing for joy,
     for you are great, O Holy One.

ISAIAH 1:18; 7:13-14; 9:2, 6-7; 12:1-6

FATHER, SON, SPIRIT

Father, I praise you. You work mighty works.

You swore to David that from the fruit of his body you would raise up the Christ to sit on his throne. You raised up Jesus and exalted him by your right hand.

I glorify you. You are the living God, who made the heaven, the earth, the sea, and all that is in them.

You have never left yourself without a witness. You did good and gave rains from the sky and fruitful seasons, filling people's hearts with food and gladness.

You are the God of glory, the Most High. You don't dwell in temples made with hands. Heaven is your throne, and the earth a footstool for your feet. What kind of house could we build for you? Your hand made all things.

Father, all of your works are known to you from eternity.

You made the world and all things in it. You are Lord of heaven and earth. You aren't served by human hands, as though you need anything, seeing as you yourself give to all life and breath, and all things.

You made from one every nation of men to live on all the surface of the earth, having determined their times and their boundaries.

You did this so they would seek you, and perhaps reach out for you and find you, though you are not far from each one of us. For in you we live, move, and have our being.

You are the Most High God; you have provided a way of salvation.

Your great grace is on me.

Father, I glorify you. I am yours.

ACTS 2:8, 11, 30-33; 4:21, 25-26, 33; 7:2, 48-50; 14:15; 15:18; 16:17; 17:24-28; 21:20; 27:23

CHRIST'S VICTORY

Father, you saved me and called me with a holy calling, not according to my works, but according to your own purpose and grace, which you gave me in Christ Jesus before times eternal.

Your purpose and grace have been revealed by the appearing of my Savior, Christ Jesus, who abolished death, and brought life and immortality to light through the good news.

I couldn't be made right with you by the works of the law, but only through faith in Jesus. So I believed in Jesus, that I might be made right with you.

I don't have any righteousness of my own from keeping the law. My only righteousness is from you through faith in Jesus.

Father, thank you for your grace which was given me in Christ. Your promise was given to me simply because I believed in Jesus. This is the work you gave me, to believe in the One you sent.

Father, thank you that I am your child through faith in Christ. I was baptized into him. I have put on him.

Because of you, Jesus, I have passed out of death into life.

What I earned through sin was death, but the Father's free gift to me is eternal life in you.

I am justified by your blood and saved from the wrath of God through you.

While I was your enemy, you reconciled me to God through your death. Now that I am reconciled, I will be saved by your life.

Where my sin abounded, your grace abounded even more. Your grace reigns through righteousness, leading to eternal life in you.

Jesus, your gift by grace overflows! Through your one act of righteousness, I have been made right with God and I have life.

To you, Father, be the glory forever and ever.

JOHN 6:29; ROMANS 5:9-10, 15, 18, 20-21; 6:23; 1 CORINTHIANS 1:3; GALATIANS 2:16; 3:22, 26-27; PHILIPPIANS 3:9; 2 TIMOTHY 1:9-10; 1 JOHN 3:14

PSALMS

God, you are my refuge and strength,
  a very present help in trouble.
Therefore I won't be afraid, though the earth changes,
    though the mountains are shaken into the heart of
      the seas;
    though its waters roar and foam,
    though the mountains tremble with their swelling.

There is a river, the streams of which make glad your city, God,
  the holy place of the Most High.
God, you are within her.
    She shall not be moved.
    You will help her at dawn.

The nations raged.
    The kingdoms tottered.
    You raised your voice, the earth melted.
Lord of hosts, you are with me.
    God of Jacob, you are my stronghold.

I behold your works, Lord,
  the desolations you have made in the earth.
You make wars cease to the end of the earth.
    You break the bow, and shatter the spear.
    You burn the chariots with fire.

You say to me,

    "Be still, and know that I am God.
        I will be exalted among the nations.
        I will be exalted in the earth."

Lord of hosts, you are with me.
    God of Jacob, you are my stronghold.

PSALM 46:1-11

THINGS TO COME

Jesus, the powers of the heavens will be shaken. Then we will see you, the Son of Man, coming in a cloud with power and great glory. Then my redemption will be near. Your kingdom will be near.

I praise you!

Heaven and earth will pass away, but your words will by no means pass away.

Jesus, in your Father's house are many dwelling places. You have gone to prepare a place for me. You will come again, and receive me to yourself, so that where you are, I may be also.

Heaven has received you until the times of restoration of all things.

You will return in the same way that you departed.

I will be with you where you are, Jesus, that I might see your glory, which the Father gave you. He loved you before the foundation of the world.

Lord, you will show wonders in the sky above,
    and signs on the earth beneath:
    blood, and fire, and billows of smoke.
The sun will be turned into darkness,
    and the moon into blood,
    before your great and glorious day comes.

Father, you have set a day in which you will judge the world in righteousness by the Man you have appointed. You gave complete assurance to everyone who he is, because you raised him from the dead.

I praise you!

LUKE 21:26-28, 31, 33; JOHN 14:2-3; 17:24; ACTS 1:11; 2:19-20; 3:25; 17:31

10TH SEVEN PRAISES

Bless the Lord, O my soul!
All that is within me,
praise his holy name!
Praise the Lord, all you works of his,
in all places of his dominion.
Praise the Lord, my soul!

PSALM 103:1, 22

THE SOVEREIGN CREATOR OF ALL

Lord, you stretch out the north over empty space,
    and hang the earth on nothing.
You bind up the waters in your thick clouds.
    You enclose the face of your throne,
    and spread your cloud on it.
On the surface of the waters you established the horizon;
    there you separate light and darkness.
The pillars of heaven tremble
    and are astonished at your rebuke.
You stir up the sea with your power;
    by your Spirit the heavens are made beautiful.
God, these are but the outskirts of your ways.
    How small a whisper do we hear of you!
    But the thunder of your power who can understand?

Spirit of God, you have made me;
    the breath of the Almighty gives me life.
I belong to you, Lord.
    You have formed me out of the clay.

God, you are mighty, and don't despise any.
    You are mighty in strength of understanding.
    You give justice to the afflicted.
You don't withdraw your eyes from the righteous,
    but you set them on thrones with kings and exalt
        them forever.

God, you send your lightning out under the whole sky,
    to the ends of the earth.
You thunder with the voice of your majesty.
    You thunder marvelously with your voice.
    You do great things, which we can't comprehend.
You say to the snow, "Fall on the earth,"
    likewise to the showers of your mighty rain.
You seal up the hand of every man,
    that all men whom you have made may know it.
I praise you, Lord!

JOB 26:7-14; 33:4,6; 36:5-7; 37:3-7

PSALMS

Clap your hands, all you nations.
  Shout to God with the voice of triumph!
You, Lord Most High, are awesome.
  You are a great King over all the earth.
You subdued nations under Israel,
  and peoples under their feet.
You chose their inheritance,
  the glory of Jacob whom you loved.
God, you have gone up with a shout,
  with the sound of a trumpet.
I sing praises to you, God! I sing praises!
  I sing praises to my King! I sing praises!
For you are the King of all the earth.
  You reign over the nations.
  You sit on your holy throne.
The shields of the earth belong to you, God.
  You are greatly exalted!
O, Lord, you are righteous.

You are my helper, God.
  You are the one who sustains my soul.
  I will give thanks to your name, Lord, for it is good.
You have delivered me out of all trouble.
  My eye has seen triumph over my enemies.

God, you are enthroned forever.
I cast my burden on you; you will sustain me.
  You will never allow the righteous to be moved.
I will trust in you.

PSALM 47:1-9; 54:4-5, 7; 55:19, 23; 129:4

THE LOVING AND FAITHFUL GOD

Lord, you are the God of my salvation,
    the rock of my strength.
    I will exalt you!
I will praise your name,
    for you have done wonderful things,
Things planned long ago,
    in complete faithfulness and truth.

Lord, you are a stronghold to the poor,
    a protector to the needy in his distress,
A refuge from the storm, a shade from the heat,
    when the blast of the ruthless is like a storm against
        the wall.

You will keep whoever's mind is steadfast in perfect peace,
    because he trusts in you.
I trust in you forever;
    you are an everlasting Rock.
You have brought down those who dwell on high, the
        lofty city.
    You lay it low, even to the ground.
    You bring it to the dust.
You are upright, Lord;
    you make the path of the righteous level.
I have waited for you.
    Your name and your renown are the desire of my soul.
With my soul I have desired you in the night.
    With my spirit within me I will seek you earnestly.
When your judgments cover the earth,
    the world's inhabitants learn righteousness.
Lord, you are majestic.

You ordain peace for me;
    you have done all my work for me.
Other lords besides you have ruled over me,
    but I will only acknowledge your name.

ISAIAH 17:10; 25:1, 4; 26:3-10, 12-13

Father, Son, Spirit

I praise you, Jesus. The highest praise to you. You are great. Blessed is your kingdom.

You are the servant whom the Father chose. You are his beloved, in whom his soul was well-pleased.

The Father put his Spirit on you. You proclaimed justice to the nations.

You did not strive, nor shout, neither did anyone hear your voice in the streets. You wouldn't break a bruised reed, nor quench a smoking flax, until you led justice to victory. In your name, the nations hope.

You had authority on earth both to forgive sins and heal. When the multitudes saw it, they marveled and glorified God.

When you entered Jerusalem as the King, humbly riding on the foal of a donkey, the multitudes kept shouting, "Hosanna to the son of David! Blessed is he who comes in the name of the Lord! Hosanna in the highest!" Out of the mouth of children you have perfected praise, Lord.

Jesus, you are the Holy One of God. You are the Father's beloved Son, the Son of the Most High God. You are seated at the right hand of the power of God.

Heaven and earth will pass away, but your words will not pass away.

You are the stone that the builders rejected, that was made the cornerstone. God did this, and it is marvelous in my eyes.

You are moved with compassion at our needs. You had compassion on the multitude, because they were like sheep without a shepherd.

You are the Son of Man. You didn't come to be served, but to serve, and to give your life as a ransom for many.

Your blood of the new covenant was poured out for many.

Jesus, I praise you!

Matthew 9:6-8; 12:18-21; 21:4-9; Mark 1:10, 24, 41; 5:7; 6:34; 10:45, 47; 11:9-10; 12:10-11; 13:31; 14:24

CHRIST'S VICTORY

Jesus, at the end of the ages, you were revealed to put away sin by the sacrifice of yourself. You offered yourself to bear my sins.

I was dead in my sins, but you have made me alive with you, having forgiven me all my transgressions.

In you, Jesus, I have redemption through your blood, the forgiveness of my trespasses.

Lord, I didn't do any work, but I believed in you who justify the ungodly. My faith was accounted for righteousness.

Thank you that my iniquities are forgiven and my sins are covered. Thank you that you will not take my sin into account!

Your blood, Jesus, cleanses me from all sin. You have been faithful and righteous to forgive me of all my sins, and to cleanse me from all unrighteousness.

You are the Righteous One. You are my Advocate with the Father, the atoning sacrifice for my sins, and not for mine only, but also for the whole world.

You have forgiven my sins for your name's sake.

Father, who can bring a charge against me, one of your chosen ones? You have justified me. Who could condemn me? Jesus is the one who died for me, and was raised from the dead for me, who is at your right hand, interceding for me.

Jesus, there is never any condemnation for me, for I am in you. In you I have redemption, the forgiveness of my sins. You have accepted me, to the glory of God.

I praise you!

ROMANS 4:5-8; 8:1, 31-32; 14:3; 15:7; EPHESIANS 1:7; COLOSSIANS 1:14; 2:13; HEBREWS 9:15, 26, 28; 1 JOHN 1:6, 9; 2:1-2

PSALMS

Lord, you are the Mighty One.
>You call the earth from sunrise to sunset.
>You shine out.
My God comes, and does not keep silent.
>A fire devours before you.
>You call to the heavens above,
>and to the earth.
The heavens declare your righteousness,
>for you yourself are judge.
You are God, my God.
>Every animal of the forest is yours,
>and the cattle on a thousand hills.
You know all the birds of the mountains.
>The wild animals of the field are yours.
If you were hungry, you would not tell me,
>for the world is yours, and all that is in it.
I offer to you the sacrifice of thanksgiving.
>I will call on you in the day of trouble.
>You will deliver me, and I will honor you.
When I offer the sacrifice of thanksgiving I glorify you,
>and prepare your way,
>so that you will show your salvation to me.

Lord, you have been a refuge for me,
>a strong tower from the enemy.
I will dwell with you forever.
>I will take refuge in the shelter of your wings.
For you have given me the heritage of those who fear
>your name.
>I will be in your presence forever.
Your lovingkindness and truth preserve me.
>So I will sing praise to your name forever.

PSALM 50:1-6, 10-15, 23; 61:3-5, 7-8

THINGS TO COME

Father, my present sufferings can't be compared with the glory you will reveal toward me. The whole creation waits eagerly for your children to be revealed.

You subjected the creation to futility, Father, in hope that one day creation itself will be delivered from its bondage. You will bring creation into the freedom of the glory of your children.

I praise you, Father!

Right now, the whole creation groans in the pangs of childbirth. I have the first fruits of the Spirit, but I groan, too. I patiently wait for my adoption, the redemption of my body.

Father, you who raised the Lord Jesus will also raise me with Jesus. For all things are for my sakes, that your grace may cause thanksgiving to abound to your glory.

Thank you that though my outer man is decaying, yet my inner man is being renewed day by day.

My temporary, light affliction is producing for me an eternal weight of glory far beyond all comparison.

Father, thank you that if the earthly house of my tent is dissolved, I have a dwelling from you, a house not made with hands, eternal, in the heavens.

I long to be clothed with my habitation from heaven, that what is mortal may be swallowed up by life. I praise you that you made me for this very thing.

Holy Spirit, you are my down payment from God, guaranteeing this.

I praise you, Lord!

ROMANS 8:18-25; 2 CORINTHIANS 4:14–5:5

11th Seven Praises

Praise the Lord!
Praise the name of the Lord;
praise him, you servants of the Lord,
you who stand in the house of the Lord,
in the courts of the house of our God!
Praise the Lord, for the Lord is good;
sing praises to his name.

PSALM 135:1-3

THE SOVEREIGN CREATOR OF ALL

Where was I when you laid the foundations of the earth, Lord?
 Did I declare its measurements?
 Did I stretch the line on it?
What were its foundations fastened on?
 Who laid its cornerstone,
When the morning stars sang together,
 and all your sons shouted for joy?
Who shut up the sea with doors,
 when it broke out of the womb,
When you made clouds its garment,
 and wrapped it in thick darkness,
 and prescribed limits for it?
You said, "You may come here, but no further.
 Your proud waves will be stopped here."
Have I commanded the morning in my days,
 and caused the dawn to rise,
 that it might take hold of the ends of the earth?
Have I entered into the springs of the sea?
 Have I walked in the recesses of the deep?
Have the gates of death been revealed to me?
 Or have I seen the gates of the shadow of death?
Have I comprehended the expanse of the earth?
 Lord, I would tell you, if I knew these things.
Where is the way to the dwelling of light?
 As for darkness, where is its place,
That I should take it to its territory,
 that I should discern the paths to its house?
Have I entered the treasuries of the snow,
 or have I seen the storehouses of the hail,
Reserved against the time of trouble,
 against the day of battle and war?
By what way is the lightning distributed,
 or the east wind scattered on the earth?
Lord, I have uttered that which I didn't understand,
 things too wonderful for me, which I didn't know.
You I praise.

JOB 38:4-24; 42:3

PSALMS

Lord, your lovingkindness endures continually.
　　I trust in your lovingkindness forever.
I will give you thanks forever for what you have done.
　　I will hope in your name, for it is good,
　　in the presence of your saints.
Lord, you are blessed!

When I am afraid, Lord,
　　I will put my trust in you.
In you, whose word I praise,
　　in you I put my trust.
I will not be afraid.
　　What can man do to me?
You count my wanderings, Lord.
　　You put my tears into your bottle.
　　Aren't they in your book?
My enemies will turn back in the day that I call on you.
　　I know this: that you are for me.
In you, God, whose word I praise,
　　I have put my trust in you.
I will not be afraid.
　　What can man do to me?
I will give thank offerings to you.
You have delivered my soul from death,
　　and prevented my feet from falling,
　　that I may walk before you in the light of the living.

Through you, God, I gain the victory;
　　you have tread down my adversaries.

I praise you, Lord!

PSALM 52:1, 8-9; 56:3-4, 8-10, 12-13; 60:12; 119:12

THE LOVING AND FAITHFUL GOD

Lord, you are the keeper of your vineyard. You water it every moment. You keep it day and night, so no one damages it. Your branch is beautiful and glorious.

The humble will rejoice in you, God; the poor among men will rejoice in you, the Holy One.

Lord, you long to be gracious to me;
>   you wait on high, exalted to show me compassion.
You are a God of justice;
>   I who wait for you in faith will be blessed.

Lord, you are gracious to me; I wait for you.
>   You are my strength every morning,
>   my salvation in the time of trouble.
At the noise of the thunder, the peoples flee.
>   When you lift yourself up, the nations are scattered.
Lord, you are exalted; you dwell on high.
>   You fill the land with justice and righteousness.
With you there is abundance of salvation, wisdom,
>   and knowledge.
>   You give your treasures to those who fear you.

Lord, you will rule in majesty.
>   You are our judge; you are our lawgiver.
>   You are our King; you will save us.

Lord, I am your redeemed, your ransomed.
>   Everlasting joy will be on my head.
I will have gladness and joy,
>   and sorrow and sighing will flee away.

In love for my soul you delivered me from the pit of corruption;
>   you have cast all my sins behind your back.
I praise you today!
>   You will save me, Lord.
I will sing songs to you all the days of my life.

ISAIAH 4:2; 27:2-3; 29:19; 30:18; 33:2-6, 21-22; 35:9-10; 38:17-20

Father, Son, Spirit

Father, you are the Creator. You are blessed forever. In creation you revealed yourself to all men. It shows your everlasting power and divinity.

Your wrath is revealed from heaven against all ungodliness and unrighteousness of men, who suppress the truth in unrighteousness.

But through the prophets in the Holy Scriptures you promised your good news concerning your Son.

You are rich in goodness, forbearance, and patience, which leads us to repentance. There is no partiality with you.

You are just, and you are the justifier of the one who has faith in Jesus.

You are the God of hope. You fill me with all joy and peace in believing, that I may abound in hope, in the power of the Holy Spirit.

Your will is good. It is well-pleasing. It is perfect.

You choose people according to your own purposes, not on the basis of works, but because of you who call.

You have mercy on whom you have mercy, and you have compassion on whom you have compassion.

You are Lord of all, abounding in riches for all who call on you. Whoever calls on your name will be saved.

You made me a living stone, part of a spiritual house, a holy priesthood, to offer up spiritual sacrifices acceptable to you through Jesus.

You made me part of a chosen race, a royal priesthood, a holy nation, a people for your own possession.

You called me out of darkness into your marvelous light. I praise you!

Romans 1:2, 18-20, 25; 2:4, 11; 3:26; 9:11, 15; 10:12-13, 20; 11:29, 12:2; 15:13; 1 Peter 2:5, 9

CHRIST'S VICTORY

Father, I praise you that because I received Jesus, I was born not of blood, nor of the will of the flesh, nor of the will of man, but of you.

How great is the love you've bestowed on me, Father, that I should be called a child of God! That's what I am. I am born of you.

I've been born of you because I have believed that Jesus is the Christ.

Jesus, you are righteous. I am born of you. I who do righteousness, am righteous, even as you are righteous.

Holy Spirit, that which is born of the flesh is flesh. That which is born of you is spirit. I am born of you.

Father, you have given me a new heart, and put a new spirit within me. You have taken away the stony heart out of my flesh, and have given me a heart of flesh. You have put your Spirit within me.

I am of you, Father. I know you, who are true. I am in him who is true, in your Son Jesus Christ.

Jesus, because I am in you, I am a new creation. The old things passed away. All things have become new. Now all things are from you.

Father of lights, I praise you! By your own will you gave birth to me by the word of truth.

I've been born again, not of corruptible seed, but of incorruptible seed, the word of God which lives and remains forever.

Jesus, thank you that I am not of the world, even as you are not of the world. I am born of you!

EZEKIEL 36:26-27; JOHN 1:12-13; 3:3, 6, 8; 17:14; 2 CORINTHIANS 5:17-18; JAMES 1:17; 1 PETER 1:23; 1 JOHN 2:29; 5:19-20

PSALMS

God, my soul takes refuge in you.
In the shadow of your wings, I will take refuge,
  until disaster has passed.
I cry out to you, Most High,
  to you who answer my requests.
You will send from heaven and save me.
  You will send out your lovingkindness and your truth.
Be exalted, God, above the heavens!
  Let your glory be above all the earth!
My heart is steadfast, God.
  My heart is steadfast.
  I will sing, yes, I will sing praises.
I will give thanks to you, Lord, among the peoples.
  I will sing praises to you among the nations.
For your great lovingkindness reaches to the heavens,
  and your truth to the skies.
Be exalted, God, above the heavens.
  Let your glory be over all the earth.

My soul rests in you alone, God.
  My salvation is from you.
You alone are my rock, my salvation, and my fortress.
  I will never be greatly shaken.
I wait in silence for you alone,
  for my expectation is from you.
You alone are my rock and my salvation, my fortress.
  I will not be shaken.
My salvation and my honor is with you, God.
  The rock of my strength, and my refuge, is in you.
I trust in you at all times;
  You are my refuge.
Power belongs to you, God,
  And lovingkindness is yours.

PSALM 57:1-3, 5, 7, 9-11; 62:1-2, 5-8, 11-12

THINGS TO COME

Father, though the number of the children of Israel are as the sand of the sea, it is the remnant who will be saved.

I praise you that you will execute your sentence on the earth quickly and in righteousness.

You, the Lord of hosts, have left Israel a seed, a posterity.

Father, by Israel's fall, salvation has come to the Gentiles. A partial hardening has happened to Israel, until the fullness of the Gentiles has come in, and so all Israel will be saved.

This is your covenant with them, Father, for the Deliverer to come out of Zion, and turn away ungodliness from Israel, when you take away their sins.

Concerning Israel's election, they are beloved for your sake, Father. For your gifts and your calling are irrevocable.

In times past, we Gentiles were disobedient to you, but now we have obtained mercy because of their disobedience.

Israel has been disobedient, that by the mercy shown to the Gentiles, Israel may also obtain mercy. For you have shut up all in disobedience, Father, that you might have mercy on all.

Oh, how deep are the riches both of your wisdom and your
      knowledge, God!
How unsearchable are your judgments,
   and unfathomable your ways!
For who has known your mind, Lord?
   Or who has been your counselor?
Or who has first given to you,
   that it might be repaid to him?
For from you, and through you, and to you are all things.
   To you be the glory forever!

ROMANS 9:27-29; 11:12, 15, 25-37

12TH SEVEN PRAISES

Always rejoice.
Pray without ceasing,
in everything give thanks,
for this is the will of God
in Christ Jesus toward you.
1 THESSALONIANS 5:16-18

THE SOVEREIGN CREATOR OF ALL

Lord, you have cut a channel for the flood water,
    a path for the thunder storm,
To cause it to rain on a land where there is no man,
    on the wilderness,
To satisfy the waste and desolate ground,
    to cause the tender grass to grow.
Doesn't the rain have a father?
    Don't you father the drops of dew?
Whose womb did the ice come out of?
    Who has given birth to the gray frost of the sky?
The waters become hard like stone,
    when the surface of the deep is frozen.
Can I bind the cluster of the Pleiades,
    or loosen the cords of Orion?
Can I lead the constellations out in their season?
    Or can I guide the Bear with her cubs?
Do I know the laws of the heavens?
    Can I establish their dominion over the earth?
Can I lift up my voice to the clouds,
    that a flood of waters may cover me?
Can I send out lightnings, that they may go forth?
    Do they report to me, "Here we are"?
Lord, who has put wisdom in the inward parts?
    Or who has given understanding to the mind?
Who can count the clouds by wisdom?
    Or who can pour out the containers of the sky?
Can I hunt the prey for the lioness,
    or satisfy the appetite of the young lions,
When they crouch in their dens,
    and lie in wait in the thicket?
Who provides for the raven his prey,
    when his young ones cry to you,
    and wander for lack of food?
Everything under the heavens is yours, Lord.
    I praise you!

JOB 38:25-41; 41:11

PSALMS

Lord, you are the God of hosts.
You laugh at my enemies.
>You scoff at all the nations.
Oh, my Strength, I watch for you,
>for you are my high tower.
You will go before me with your lovingkindness.
>You will let me look at my enemies in triumph.
You are my shield.
>You rule to the ends of the earth.
I will sing of your strength;
>I will sing aloud of your lovingkindness in the morning.
For you have been my high tower,
>a refuge in the day of my distress.
To you, my Strength, I will sing praises.
>For you are my high tower, the God of my mercy.

God, you are my God.
>I have seen your power and your glory.
Because your lovingkindness is better than life,
>my lips will praise you.
I will bless you while I live.
>I will lift up my hands in your name.
>My soul shall be satisfied as with the richest food.
My mouth will praise you with joyful lips,
>when I remember you on my bed,
>and think about you in the night watches.
For you have been my help.
>I will rejoice in the shadow of your wings.
My soul stays close to you.
>Your right hand holds me up.
I will rejoice in you.
>Everyone who swears by you will praise you.

PSALM 59:5, 8-11, 13, 16-17; 63:1, 3-8, 11

The Loving and Faithful God

Jesus, the voice in the wilderness called out,

> "Prepare the way of the Lord,
> > make a level highway in the desert for our God.
> Every valley shall be exalted,
> > and every mountain and hill shall be made low.
> The Lord's glory will be revealed,
> > and all people will see it together;
> For the mouth of the Lord has spoken it."

Those who told good news to Zion went up on a high mountain.
Those who told good news to Jerusalem lifted up their voice
> with strength!
They said to the cities of Judah, "Behold, your God!"

Lord, all flesh is like grass,
> and all its glory is like the flower of the field.
The grass withers, the flower fades,
> because your breath, Lord, blows on it.
Surely the people are like grass.
> The grass withers, the flower fades;
> but the word of my God stands forever.

Lord, you have chosen me and not rejected me.
> You are with me. I won't be afraid.
> You are my God. I won't be dismayed.
> You will strengthen me.
> You will help me.
> You will uphold me with the right hand of your
> > righteousness.
All those who rage against me will be disappointed and
> confounded.
> Those who strive with me will be like nothing, and
> > will perish.
> Those who war against me will be as nothing.
You are my God; you will hold my right hand,
> and say to me, "Don't be afraid. I will help you."

Isaiah 40:1-9; 41:9-13

FATHER, SON, SPIRIT

Jesus, you are the Christ of God, the Holy One of God, the Son of the Most High.

You are mightier than any other, the strap of whose sandals even John the Baptist was not worthy to untie.

You are the Son of David. God has given you the throne of David, and you will reign over the house of Jacob forever. There will be no end to your kingdom.

All things were handed over to you by your Father. No one knows who the Father is, except you, and those you choose to reveal him to. Whoever knows you knows the Father also.

Thank you that you have made the Father known to me, and you will continue to make him known to me.

Jesus, all things that were written through the prophets concerning you were completed.

You were delivered up to the Gentiles, mocked, treated shamefully, and spit on. They scourged you and killed you. On the third day, you rose again.

You are the bridegroom. You come from heaven, from the Father, and are above all.

You laid down your life, that you might take it up again. No one took it away from you, but you laid it down by yourself. You had power to lay it down, and you had power to take it up again.

Jesus, I didn't choose you, but you chose me. I am not of the world. You chose me out of the world.

You give me your peace. What you give isn't like what the world gives. In you I have peace.

Jesus, I praise you!

LUKE 1:32-33; 3:16; 4:34; 8:28; 9:20; 10:22; 18:31-33, 38; JOHN 3:27; 7:41; 8:20; 10:17-18; 13:1; 14:27; 15:16, 19; 16:28, 33; 17:26

CHRIST'S VICTORY

Father, you have made me your beloved child.

I am a child of promise, your heir.

I praise you that when the fullness of the time came, you sent your Son. Jesus redeemed me so I could be adopted by you as your child.

Because I'm your child, you sent the Spirit of your Son into my heart, crying, "Abba, Father!"

I'm not a slave anymore; I'm a son. And if I'm a son, then I'm your heir through Christ!

Holy Spirit, you are the Spirit of adoption. I didn't receive a spirit of slavery that produces fear. I received you. By you I cry out to God, "Abba! Father!"

You testify along with my own spirit that I am God's child. I am his heir, a joint heir with Christ.

Jesus, you have made me a fellow heir with you.

In you there is neither Jew nor Greek, neither slave nor free man, neither male nor female; we are all one in you. If we are yours, we are Abraham's offspring, and we are heirs according to God's promise.

Jesus, thank you that even though a bondservant doesn't live in the house forever, a son does. You have made me a son. You make me free, and I am free indeed.

Father, you have called those who weren't your people, your people, and those who were not your beloved, beloved. I was not yours, but now I am a child of the living God.

I am your holy and beloved one.

Father, I praise you!

JOHN 8:35-36; ROMANS 8:15-17; 9:25-26; GALATIANS 3:28-29; 4:4-7, 28-30; EPHESIANS 3:6; 5:1; COLOSSIANS 3:12

PSALMS

Lord, all mankind will declare your work,
    and ponder what you have done.
The righteous will be glad in you,
    and will take refuge in you.
    All the upright in heart will praise you!

Make a joyful shout to God, all the earth!
    Sing to the glory of his name!
    Offer glory and praise!
God, how awesome are your deeds!
    Through the greatness of your power,
    your enemies submit themselves to you.
All the earth will worship you
    and will sing to you;
    they will sing to your name.
Come, and see God's deeds—
    your awesome work, Lord, on behalf of the children
        of men.
You turned the sea into dry land.
    Your people went through the river on foot.
    They rejoiced in you.
You rule by your might forever.
    Your eyes watch the nations.
Praise our God, you peoples!
    Make the sound of his praise heard,
Who preserves our life among the living,
    and doesn't allow our feet to be moved.
For you, God, have refined us, as silver is refined.
    You brought us to the place of abundance.
    Come and hear, all you who fear God.
Lord, I will declare what you have done for my soul.
    I extol you with my tongue.
I bless you, God, for you have not turned away my prayer,
    nor your lovingkindness from me.

I praise you!

PSALM 64:9-10; 66:1-7, 9-11, 16-17, 20

THINGS TO COME

Jesus, every man will stand before your judgment seat.

At your name, every knee will bow, those in heaven, those on earth, and those under the earth. And every tongue will confess that you are Lord, to the glory of God the Father.

Jesus, you will bring about your appearing at the proper time.

When you come, you will both bring to light the hidden things of darkness, and reveal the counsels of men's hearts. Then each man will get his praise from God.

Father, I praise you that I and all the saints will judge the world. We will even judge angels!

You raised up the Lord, and you will also raise me up by your power.

Thank you for the hope laid up for me in the heavens, which I heard in the word of the truth, the good news.

Jesus, where there are prophecies, they will be done away with. Where there are various tongues, they will cease. Where there is knowledge, it will be done away with.

I know in part and prophesy in part; but when that which is complete has come, then the partial will be done away with.

Now I see in a mirror, dimly, but then face to face. Now I know in part, but then I will know fully, even as I have been fully known.

Jesus, I praise you!

ROMANS 14:10-11; PHILIPPIANS 2:10-11; 1 CORINTHIANS 4:5; 6:1-3, 14; 13:9-12; COLOSSIANS 1:5; 1 TIMOTHY 6:14

13TH SEVEN PRAISES

*Whoever offers the sacrifice of
thanksgiving glorifies me,
and prepares his way so that
I will show God's salvation to him.*

PSALM 50:23

THE SOVEREIGN CREATOR OF ALL

Lord, do I know the time when the mountain goats give birth?
  Do I watch when the doe bears fawns?
Can I count the months that they fulfill?
  Or do I know the time when they give birth?
They bow themselves; they bear their young;
  they end their labor pains.
Their young ones become strong.
  They grow up in the open field.
  They go out, and don't return again.
Who has set the wild donkey free?
  Or who has loosened the bonds of the swift donkey,
Whose home you have made the wilderness,
  and the salt land his dwelling place?
The range of the mountains is his pasture;
  he searches after every green thing.
Will the wild ox be content to serve me, Lord?
  Or will he stay by my feeding trough?
Can I hold the wild ox in the furrow with his harness?
  Or will he till the valleys after me?
Will I trust him, because his strength is great?
  Or will you leave to him my labor?
The wings of the ostrich wave proudly;
  she leaves her eggs on the earth,
  warms them in the dust,
And forgets that the foot may crush them,
  or that the wild animal may trample them.
She deals harshly with her young ones, as if they were not hers.
  Though her labor is in vain, she is without fear,
Because you have deprived her of wisdom,
  neither have you imparted to her understanding.

Lord, everything under the heavens is yours.
  I know that you can do all things,
  and that no purpose of yours can be thwarted.

I praise you!

Job 39:1-6, 8-17; 41:11; 42:2

PSALMS

Praise waits for you, God, in Zion.
>All men will come to you—you who hear prayer.
>You are the one who atoned for our transgressions.
Blessed is the one whom you choose and cause to come near.
>I will be filled with the goodness of your house.
By awesome deeds of righteousness, you answer me,
>God of my salvation.

You are the hope of all the ends of the earth,
>of those who are far away on the sea.
By your power, you form the mountains.
>You arm yourself with strength.
You still the roaring of the seas,
>the roaring of their waves,
>and the turmoil of the nations.

The whole earth is filled with awe at your wonders.
>You call the morning's dawn and the evening with songs
>>of joy.
You visit the earth, and water it.
>You greatly enrich it.
The river of God is full of water.
>You provide grain, for so you have ordained it.
You crown the year with your bounty.
>Your carts overflow with abundance.
The wilderness grasslands overflow.
>The hills are clothed with gladness.
The pastures are covered with flocks.
>The valleys also are clothed with grain.
They shout for joy!
>They also sing.

O Lord, my God, I praise you!

PSALM 65:1-9, 11-13

THE LOVING AND FAITHFUL GOD

Lord, I will rejoice in you.
    I will glory in the Holy One.
You answer the poor and needy.
    You will not forsake them.

Jesus, you are the Servant whom the Father upheld,
    his chosen, in whom his soul delights.
He put his Spirit on you.
    You will bring justice to the nations.
You did not shout,
    nor raise your voice,
    nor cause it to be heard in the street.
You won't break a bruised reed.
    You won't quench a dimly burning wick.
    You faithfully bring justice.
You will not fail nor be discouraged,
    until you have set justice in the earth.
Lord God, you created the heavens and stretched them out.
    You spread out the earth and that which comes out of it.
    You give breath to its people and spirit to those who
        walk on it.
You called Jesus in righteousness.
    You held his hand.
You kept him, and made him a covenant for the people,
    as a light for the nations, to open the blind eyes,
    to bring the prisoners out of the dungeon,
    and those who sit in darkness out of the prison.
You are the I AM.
    That is your name.
You will not give your glory to another,
    nor your praise to engraved images.
Lord, the former things you declared happened.
    Now you declare new things.
    You tell us of them before they come to pass.

I praise you!

Isaiah 41:16-17; 42:1-9

FATHER, SON, SPIRIT

Holy Spirit, you are the Spirit of truth. You have come and you guide us into all truth.

You don't speak from yourself, but whatever you hear, you speak. You declare to us the things to come.

You glorify Jesus, for you take what is his and declare it to us.

You teach us all things. Jesus sent you from the Father, and you testify about him.

Holy Spirit, you search all things, even the deep things of God. No one knows the things of God, except you.

I have received, not the spirit of the world, but I have received you, Holy Spirit.

You are from God. You have come so I might know the things that God has freely given me.

For those who love him, the Father has prepared things which eyes have not seen and ears have not heard, which haven't entered into the heart of man. Spirit, you have revealed these things to us.

Thank you that I have the mind of Christ.

You are my anointing from the Holy One. You remain in me, and you teach me concerning all things. By you I know the truth.

You are true. By you I know that I remain in Jesus and he in me.

You tell me God has made a new covenant. You tell me that God has put his laws into my heart, and has written them on my mind. You tell me that God won't remember my sins anymore.

Holy Spirit, I praise you!

JOHN 16:13-14; 1 CORINTHIANS 2:9-12, 16; HEBREWS 10:15-17; 1 JOHN 2:20-21, 27; 4:13

CHRIST'S VICTORY

Jesus, you and the Father are one. He is in you, and you are in him.

On earth you lived because of him.

You could do nothing of yourself. You only did what you saw the Father doing.

You could do nothing of yourself. As you heard, you judged, and your judgment was righteous, because you didn't seek your own will, but the Father's.

You did nothing of yourself, but as the Father taught you, you spoke. As the Father said to you, you spoke.

You didn't speak from yourself, but the Father who lived in you did his works.

Jesus, you are in the Father, and the Father is in you. You and the Father are one.

I am one with you and the Father. You are in me, and I am in you.

I am one spirit with you.

Jesus, because you live, I also live. As you lived because of the Father, so I live because of you. I am in you, and you are in me.

It is no longer I who live, but you live in me.

You are the true vine. I live in you. You live in me. Apart from you I can do nothing.

Jesus, as you are, so also am I in this world.

I praise you, Jesus!

JOHN 5:19, 28-30; 6:57; 8:27; 10:30, 38; 14:6, 10-11, 19-20; 15:1-5; 17:20-23; ROMANS 8:10; 1 CORINTHIANS 6:17; GALATIANS 2:20; COLOSSIANS 3:4; 1 JOHN 4:17

Psalms

Let the peoples praise you, God.
    Let all the peoples praise you,
That your way may be known on earth,
    and your salvation among all nations.
Let the nations be glad and sing for joy,
    for you will judge the peoples with equity,
    and govern the nations on earth.
Let the peoples praise you, God.
    Let all the peoples praise you.
The earth has yielded its increase.
    You, God, even my God, will bless us.
All the ends of the earth shall fear you.

Lord, your lovingkindness is good,
    your compassion abundant.
I will praise your name with a song,
    and will magnify you with thanksgiving.
Let heaven and earth praise you;
    the seas, and everything that moves in them!

You are good to me, God.
    I am continually with you.
    You hold my right hand.
You will guide me with your counsel,
    and afterward receive me to glory.
Whom have I in heaven but you?
    There is no one on earth I desire besides you.
My flesh and my heart may fail,
    but you are the strength of my heart and my portion
        forever.
Your nearness is my good, Lord.
    I have made you my refuge,
    that I may tell of all your works.

Psalm 67:3-7; 69:16, 30, 34; 73:1, 23-28

THINGS TO COME

Jesus, you have been raised from the dead. You became the first fruits of those who are asleep.

Since death came by man, the resurrection of the dead also came by man. As in Adam all die, so also in you all will be made alive.

You were the first fruits. Then will be those who are yours, at your coming.

Then the end comes, when you will deliver up the kingdom to God, even the Father, when you will have abolished all rule and all authority and power.

For you must reign until you have put all your enemies under your feet. The last enemy that will be abolished is death.

When all things have been subjected to you, then you will also be subjected to him who subjected all things to you, that God may be all in all.

Jesus, flesh and blood can't inherit God's kingdom; nor can the perishable inherit the imperishable.

We will not all sleep, but we will all be changed, in a moment, in the twinkling of an eye, at the last trumpet. For the trumpet will sound and the dead will be raised incorruptible, and we will be changed.

This perishable body must become imperishable, and this mortal must put on immortality.

When this perishable body becomes imperishable, and this mortal puts on immortality, then what is written will happen:

> "Death is swallowed up in victory.
> Death, where is your sting?
> Death, where is your victory?"

How I thank you, Father! You give me the victory through my Lord Jesus Christ.

1 CORINTHIANS 15:20-28, 50-57

14th Seven Praises

I will sing to the Lord as long as I live.
I will sing praise to my God while I have my being.
Bless the Lord, O my soul.
Praise the Lord!

Psalm 104:33, 35

THE SOVEREIGN CREATOR OF ALL

Lord, have I given the horse might?
   Have I clothed his neck with a quivering mane?
Have I made him leap as a locust?
   The glory of his snorting is awesome.
   He paws in the valley, and rejoices in his strength.
He eats up the ground with fierceness and rage,
   neither does he stand still at the sound of the trumpet.
Is it by my wisdom that the hawk soars,
   and stretches her wings toward the south?
Is it at my command that the eagle mounts up,
   and makes his nest on high?
On the cliff he dwells, and makes his home,
   on the point of the cliff, the stronghold.
I look at the behemoth, which you made as well as me.
   His strength is in his thighs; he moves his tail like a cedar.
His bones are like tubes of bronze.
   His limbs are like bars of iron.
He is the chief of your works, God.
   You made him and give him his sword.
Shall any take him when he is on the watch,
   or pierce through his nose with a snare?
Can I draw out leviathan with a fish hook,
   or press down his tongue with a cord?
If I laid my hand on him,
   I would remember the battle, and not do it again!
   I wouldn't dare stir him up.

Who can stand before you, Lord?
   Who has first given to you, that you should repay him?
Will I annul your judgments?
   Will I condemn you, that I may be justified?
Do I have an arm like you, God?
   Can I thunder with a voice like you?
   My own right hand can't save me.

You are the one I praise!

JOB 39:19-22, 24, 26-29; 40:8-9, 14-20, 23-24; 41:1-2, 8, 10-11

PSALMS

Let the righteous be glad, Lord.
I rejoice before you; yes, I rejoice with gladness.
I sing to you! I sing praises to your name!
I extol you who ride on the clouds:
To the I AM, your name! I rejoice before you!
A father of the fatherless, and a defender of widows,
are you, God, in your holy habitation.
You set the lonely in families.
You bring out the prisoners with singing.
God, when you went out before your people,
when you marched through the wilderness, at your presence
the earth trembled and the sky also poured down rain.
You confirmed your inheritance when it was weary.
You, God, prepared your goodness for the poor.
You announced your word.
The ones who proclaim it are a great company.
Lord, you will dwell forever.
Your chariots, God, are tens of thousands and thousands
of thousands.
You are among them.
You have ascended on high; you have led away captives.
Blessed be you, Lord, who daily bears our burdens,
even the God who is our salvation.
You are to us a God of deliverance.
To you, Lord, belongs escape from death.
I bless you in the congregation,
even you, Lord, in the assembly!
God, you have commanded your strength.
Sing to God, you kingdoms of the earth!
I sing praises to you, Lord,
To you who ride on the heaven of heavens, which are of old;
you utter your voice, a mighty voice.
Ascribe strength to God! Your strength is in the skies.
You are awesome, God, in your sanctuaries.
You give strength and power to your people.
Praise be to you, God!

PSALM 68:3-12, 17-20, 26, 28, 32-35

THE LOVING AND FAITHFUL GOD

Lord, you created me and formed me.
You tell me not to be afraid, for you have redeemed me.
    You have called me by name.
    I am yours.
When I pass through the waters, you will be with me,
    and through the rivers, they will not overflow me.
When I walk through the fire, I will not be burned,
    and flame will not scorch me.
For you are the Lord my God,
    the Holy One, my Savior.
I am precious and honored in your sight,
    and you have loved me.
I won't be afraid, for you are with me.
    I am called by your name;
    you created me for your glory;
    you formed me; yes, you made me.

Lord, we are your witnesses,
    that we may know and believe you,
    and understand that you are he.
Before you there was no God formed,
    neither will there be after you.
You yourself are the Lord.
    Besides you, there is no savior.
You have declared, you have saved, and you have shown.
    Therefore, I am your witness, and you are God.
    Forever you are he.
There is no one who can deliver out of your hand.
    You will act; who can prevent it?
You are the Lord, my Holy One, my Creator, my King.

You are the one who blots out my transgressions for your
      own sake;
    you will not remember my sins.

I praise you!

ISAIAH 43:1-7, 10-15, 25

Father, Son, Spirit

You are the God and Father of my Lord Jesus Christ. You are blessed forevermore.

You have called me and made me a saint. You love me.

Father, I love you. I am known by you.

Because of you, I am in Christ Jesus. He is my wisdom from you, my righteousness, my sanctification, my redemption.

The earth is yours, Father, with all its fullness. Everything I have, I have received from you.

There is only one God—you, Father. All things are from you, and I exist for you. And there is only one Lord, Jesus Christ, through whom are all things, and I live through him.

Father, you are the head of Christ. I am the image and glory of you.

You are the Father of mercies and God of all comfort. You comfort me in all my affliction with a comfort that abounds through Christ.

Father, I don't trust in myself, but in you who raise the dead. On you I have set my hope, that you will deliver me. You are faithful.

You have shone in my heart to give the light of knowing your glory in the face of Christ.

You establish me in Christ and anoint me. You sealed me and gave me the down payment of the Spirit in my heart. Your kingdom is not in word, but in power.

Father, I may have nothing, yet I possess all things.

You are the God of peace. You are the God of love. If anyone boasts, may he boast in you. You raised Jesus from the dead.

With my mouth I glorify you, God and Father of my Lord Jesus Christ.

Thanks be to you for your unspeakable gift!

Romans 1:7; 15:6; 1 Corinthians 1:30-31; 4:7, 20; 8:3, 6; 10:13, 30; 11:3, 7; 14:33; 2 Corinthians 1:3-5, 9-10, 18, 22-23; 4:6; 6:10; 9:15; 10:17; 11:31; 13:11; Galatians 1:1

CHRIST'S VICTORY

Father, I praise you that you have made known to me the glorious riches of the mystery which was hidden for ages and generations, but now has been revealed: Christ in me.

You have put this treasure in me, a clay vessel, so that the exceeding greatness of the power may be of you, and not from me.

Jesus, you are the image of God. The gospel is the good news of your glory. You are the light shining out of darkness.

You have shone inside my heart, to bring the light of knowing God's glory in the face of Christ.

Father, it was your good pleasure to reveal your Son in me.

Jesus, I am pressed on every side, yet not crushed; perplexed, yet not despairing; pursued, yet not forsaken; struck down, yet not destroyed; always carrying in my body your dying, that your life may be revealed in my body.

I am always delivered to death for your sake, Jesus, that your life may be revealed in my mortal flesh.

It is no longer I who live, but you live in me.

My boasting is in you, Jesus. I don't speak of anything except what you have accomplished through me.

Jesus, you are powerful in me. For you were crucified through weakness, yet you live through the power of God. Thank you that you are in me.

For me, to live is you.

You are the life. You are my life.

JOHN 14:6; ROMANS 15:17-18; 2 CORINTHIANS 4:4-11; 13:3-5; GALATIANS 1:15-16; 2:20; PHILIPPIANS 1:21; COLOSSIANS 1:25-27; 3:4

PSALMS

In you, Lord, I take refuge.
>You are my rock and my fortress.
You are my hope, Lord God,
>my confidence from my youth.
I have relied on you from the womb.
>You are he who took me out of my mother's womb.
I will always praise you.
>You are my strong refuge.
My mouth will be filled with your praise,
>with your honor all day long.
I will always hope,
>and will praise you more and more.
My mouth will tell about your righteousness,
>and of your salvation all day,
>though I don't know its full measure.
I will proclaim your mighty acts, Lord.
>I will tell of your righteousness, even of yours alone.
God, you have taught me from my youth.
>I have declared your wondrous works.
I will declare your strength to the next generation,
>your might to everyone who is to come.
God, your righteousness reaches to the heavens.
>You have done great things.
>Who is like you?
I will praise you for your faithfulness, my God.
>I sing praises to you, Holy One.
My lips will shout for joy!
>My soul, which you have redeemed, sings praises to you!
My tongue will also talk about your righteousness all day long.

Praise be to you, Lord;
>you alone do marvelous deeds.
Praise be to your glorious name forever;
>may the whole earth be filled with your glory.

PSALM 71:1-8, 14-24; 72:18-19

THINGS TO COME

Jesus, thank you that my citizenship is in heaven. I await you from there, my Savior.

You will change my weak and mortal body into a glorious body like yours, according to the power you have to subject all things to yourself.

Thank you that by your grace my name is written in the book of life.

Thank you that I will receive the reward of the inheritance.

Father, I wait for your Son from heaven, whom you raised from the dead: Jesus, who delivers me from the wrath to come.

Jesus, I believe that you died and rose again. Even so God will bring with you those who have fallen asleep in you.

I look for the blessed hope and the appearing of your glory—my great God and Savior, Jesus Christ. You are the one who gave yourself for me.

You promised that we who are alive, who are left until your coming, will not precede those who have fallen asleep.

You yourself will descend from heaven with a shout, with the voice of the archangel and with God's trumpet.

The dead in Christ will rise first, then we who are alive, who are left, will be caught up together with them in the clouds, to meet you in the air.

So we will be with you forever.

I praise you!

PHILIPPIANS 3:20-21; 4:3; COLOSSIANS 3:24; 1 THESSALONIANS 1:10; 4:14-17; 1 PETER 1:6; 4:12

15th Seven Praises

Jehoshaphat appointed men to sing to the Lord and to praise him for the splendor of his holiness as they went out at the head of the army, saying: "Give thanks to the Lord, for his love endures forever." As they began to sing and praise, the Lord set ambushes against the men of Ammon and Moab and Mount Seir who were invading Judah, and they were defeated.

2 Chronicles 20:21-22, NIV

THE SOVEREIGN CREATOR OF ALL

Lord, you are clothed with the glory of your majesty!
    The proud looks of man will be brought low,
    the arrogance of men will be bowed down;
    you alone will be exalted.

You are the Lord of hosts. You command armies. You will
be exalted in judgment. You, the Holy One, are set apart
in righteousness.

Lord, Isaiah saw you sitting on a throne, high and lifted up;
and your train filled the temple. Above you stood seraphim,
each with six wings. With two they covered their face, with
two they covered their feet, and with two they flew. One
called to another, and said,

    "Holy, holy, holy, is the Lord of hosts!
    The whole earth is full of his glory!"

The foundations of the thresholds shook at the voice of him
who called, and the temple was filled with smoke.

Lord, you are the King, God of the heavenly armies!

You remove the boundaries of nations and rob their riches.
Like a conqueror you bring down their rulers.

Like one gathers eggs that are abandoned, you gather all
the earth.

You have determined a plan for the whole earth. Your hand
is stretched out over all the nations. For you, God of hosts,
have planned, and who can stop it? Your hand is stretched
out, and who can turn it back?

By the strength of your hand you accomplish it, and by your
wisdom and understanding.

Lord, in the day to come, people will look to you, their
Maker, and their eyes will depend on the Holy One.

You are glorified!

Isaiah 2:10-11; 5:16; 6:1-5; 10:13-14; 14:26-27; 17:7; 26:15

Psalms

God, you are my King of old,
  working salvation throughout the earth.
The day is yours, the night is also yours.
  You have prepared the light and the sun.
You have set all the boundaries of the earth.
  You have made summer and winter.

I give thanks to you, God.
  I give thanks, for your name is near.
  I tell about your wondrous works.
When you choose the appointed time,
  you will judge blamelessly.
The earth and all its inhabitants quake.
  You firmly hold its pillars.
God, you are the judge.
  You put down one and lift up another.
I will sing praises to you forever.

God, you are known.
  Your name is great.
You are resplendent,
  more majestic than the mountains.
You, even You, are to be feared;
  who may stand in Your presence?
You caused judgment to be heard from heaven;
  the earth feared and was still
  when you arose to judgment,
  to save all the humble of the earth.
You are feared by the kings of the earth.

I sing aloud to you, God, my strength!
  I make a joyful shout to you!

Psalm 74:12, 16-17; 75:1-3, 7-9; 76:1-4, 7-9, 12; 81:1

THE LOVING AND FAITHFUL GOD

Lord, you pour water on the one who is thirsty,
  and streams on the dry ground.
You pour your Spirit on us,
  your blessing on our offspring.
I am yours.

Lord, you have formed me.
  You have promised, "I will not forget you."
You have blotted out my sins as a thick cloud.
  You have redeemed me.
 Sing, you heavens, for the Lord has done it!
  Shout, you lower parts of the earth!
  Break out into singing, you mountains,
O forest, all of your trees,
  for the Lord has redeemed and will glorify himself!
Lord, you are my Redeemer who formed me from the womb.
  You are God, who makes all things;
  who alone stretches out the heavens;
Who spreads out the earth by yourself;
  who turns wise men backward,
  and makes their knowledge foolish;
Who confirms the word of your servant,
  and fulfills the pronouncements of your messengers.

Lord, you have carried me from my birth,
  from the womb.
Even to my old age you are he,
  and even to my gray hairs you will carry me.
You made me; you will bear me up.
  You will carry me and will deliver me.

O Lord, you are my Redeemer.
  The Lord of Armies is your name.
You are the Holy One.

ISAIAH 44:3,5, 21-26; 46:3-4; 47:4

FATHER, SON, SPIRIT

Jesus, you are the Christ, God's Son, the one who came into the world. You are the true bread out of heaven.

Whoever feeds on you will live because of you. The food you give me remains to eternal life. You will raise me up on the last day. I will live forever.

Before Abraham came into existence, you are. Abraham saw your day. Isaiah saw your glory, and spoke of you.

But you didn't seek your own glory. You only sought the glory of the One who sent you. You honored the Father. There was no unrighteousness in you.

You glorified the Father on earth. You accomplished the work he gave you to do.

You loved the Father, so you did what he told you to do.

Then the Father glorified you with the glory you had with him before the world ever existed.

All things that are yours are the Father's, and all things that are the Father's are yours. In this you are glorified.

Jesus, you know the Father. No one has seen the Father except the One who is from God. You have seen him.

You were from him, and he sent you. The works that he gave you to do show that he sent you.

You came down from heaven, not to do your will, but the will of your Father who sent you. You always did the things that were pleasing to him.

Jesus, no one can come to you, unless it has been given to you by your Father. No one can come to you unless the Father who sent you draws him, and you will raise him up on the last day.

You are the Son of Man. The Father glorified you, and the Father was glorified in you.

I praise you, Jesus!

JOHN 5:32, 35-36; 6:27, 38, 44, 46, 56-58, 65; 7:18, 29; 8:29, 49-50, 56, 58; 11:27; 12:41; 13:31; 14:31; 17:1, 4-5, 10

CHRIST'S VICTORY

Jesus, I am one with you. I am in you. You are in me. I am one spirit with you.

You were nailed to a cross and put to death.

I died with you.

I was buried with you and raised with you through faith in the working of God, who raised you from the dead.

You died for all, therefore all died.

I have been crucified with you.

My old man was crucified with you.

I died to sin.

I died to the elementary principles of the world.

Through your body, I died to the law, so that I might live to God.

Through your cross, the world has been crucified to me, and I to the world.

Jesus, the Father raised you from the dead.

You raised me up with you.

I am alive to you. I will live with you.

It is no longer I who live, but you live in me.

I died, and my life is hidden with you in God. You are my life.

Jesus, I praise you!

JOHN 14:20; 17:21; ACTS 2:23; ROMANS 6:1, 6, 8; 7:4; 1 CORINTHIANS 6:17; 2 CORINTHIANS 5:11; GALATIANS 2:19-20; 6:14; EPHESIANS 1:20; COLOSSIANS 2:12-13, 20; 3:1-4

PSALMS

I will remember your deeds, Lord.
    I will remember your wonders of old.
I will also meditate on all your work,
    and consider your doings.
Your way, God, is holy.
    What god is great like you?
You are the God who does wonders.
    You have made your strength known among the peoples.
    You have redeemed your people with your arm.
The waters saw you, God.
    The waters saw you, and they writhed.
    The depths also convulsed.
The clouds poured out water.
    The skies resounded with thunder.
    Your arrows also flashed.
The voice of your thunder was in the whirlwind.
    The lightnings lit up the world.
    The earth trembled and shook.
Your way was through the sea;
    your paths through the great waters.
    Your footsteps were not known.
You led your people like a flock,
    by the hand of Moses and Aaron.

Lord, I will tell to the generation to come your praises,
    your strength and your wondrous deeds that you
        have done.
    You are my rock.
God, Most High, you are my Redeemer,
    the Holy One.

PSALM 77:11-20; 78:4, 35

THINGS TO COME

Lord Jesus, you will be revealed from heaven with your mighty angels in flaming fire, punishing those who don't know God, and those who don't obey your good news.

They will pay the penalty of eternal destruction, away from your presence and from the glory of your might.

You will come on that day to be glorified in your saints and to be marveled at by all those who have believed.

You will come back and gather us to yourself after the rebellion comes, and the man of sin is revealed, the son of destruction.

You will slay him with the breath of your mouth, and destroy him by the appearance of your coming.

Jesus, I know whom I have believed, and I am convinced that you are able to guard that which I have committed to you for that day.

You are the Lord Jesus Christ. You will judge the living and the dead at your appearing and your kingdom.

Jesus, the crown of righteousness is stored up for me, which you, Righteous Judge, will give to me on that day; and not to me only, but also to all those who have loved your appearing.

At the revelation of your glory I will rejoice with exceeding joy. The Spirit of glory and of God rests on me.

I praise you!

2 THESSALONIANS 1:7; 2:1, 3, 8; 2 TIMOTHY 1:12; 4:1, 8; TITUS 2:13-14

16TH SEVEN PRAISES

Praise the Lord!
Sing to the Lord a new song,
his praise in the assembly of the saints.
Let the high praises of God be in their mouths,
and a two-edged sword in their hand,
to execute vengeance on the nations
and punishments on the peoples,
to bind their kings with chains,
and their nobles with fetters of iron;
to execute on them the written judgment.
All his saints have this honor.
Praise the Lord!

Psalm 149:1, 6-8

THE SOVEREIGN CREATOR OF ALL

Lord, you, the God of the heavenly armies, will become a crown of glory and a diadem of beauty to the remnant of your people.

I will see your glory, the excellence of my God.

God of the Armies, you are enthroned among the cherubim. You are the God, even you alone, of all the kingdoms of the earth. You have made heaven and earth.

The gods of the peoples are no gods, but the work of men's hands, wood and stone. But you are my God. You will save, that all the kingdoms of the earth may know that you are God, even you only.

Men go into the caverns of the ragged rocks,
    from before your terror,
    and from the glory of your majesty,
    when you arise to shake the earth mightily.

I lift up my voice. I shout for your majesty, Lord. I glorify you, even the name of I AM. From the uttermost part of the earth have I heard songs of glory.

Lord, you are the one who comforts me.
    I will not be afraid of man who will die,
    and of the son of man who will be made like grass.
I have not forgotten you, my Maker,
    who stretched out the heavens,
    and laid the foundations of the earth.
You are the Lord my God, who stirs up the sea
      so that its waves roar.
    The God of Armies is your name.
You have put your words in my mouth
    and have covered me in the shadow of your hand,
That you may plant the heavens,
    and lay the foundations of the earth,
    and tell me I am yours.

ISAIAH 2:21; 24:14-15; 28:5-6; 35:2; 37:15-16, 19-20; 51:12-16

PSALMS

Lord, I am a sheep of your pasture.
 I will give you thanks forever.
 I will praise you forever, to all generations.

You preside in the great assembly.
 You judge among the gods.

You will judge the earth,
 for you inherit all of the nations.

Lord, you alone, whose name is I AM,
 are the Most High over all the earth.

How lovely are your dwellings,
 Lord God of hosts!
My soul longs and even faints for your courts.
 My heart and my flesh cry out for the living God.
Yes, the sparrow has found a home,
 and the swallow a nest for herself,
 where she may have her young,
 near your altars, Lord of hosts, my King, and my God.
Blessed are those who dwell in your house.
 They are always praising you.
Blessed are those whose strength is in you.
 You are my shield.
A day in your courts is better than a thousand outside.
 I would rather be a doorkeeper in your house
  than to dwell in the tents of wickedness.
For you, God, are a sun and a shield.
 You give grace and glory.
 You withhold no good thing from me.
Lord of hosts,
 I am blessed, for I have put my trust in you.

PSALM 79:13; 82:1, 8; 83:18; 84:1-5, 9-12

THE LOVING AND FAITHFUL GOD

You are the Lord.
 There is no other.
You have not spoken in secret,
 in a land of darkness.
You didn't tell me to seek you in vain.
You speak righteousness;
 you declare things that are right.
Who has shown things from ancient times?
 Who has declared it of old?
 Haven't you, God?
There is no other God besides you, a just God and a Savior.
 There is no one besides you.
All the ends of the earth look to you and are saved;
 you are God, and there is no other.
You have sworn by yourself.
The word has gone out of your mouth in righteousness,
 and will not be revoked,
That to you every knee shall bow,
 every tongue shall take an oath.
They will say of you,
 "There is righteousness and strength only in God."
To you will men come.
 All those who raged against you will be put to shame.
In you all of your offspring will be justified,
 and will rejoice!

Lord, you are my Redeemer, the Holy One.
You are the Lord my God;
 you teach me to profit,
 and lead me by the way that I should go.

You are my Lord. I, who wait for you, will not be
disappointed. All people will know that you are our Savior
and our Redeemer, the Mighty One.

ISAIAH 45:18-25; 48:17; 49:23, 26

FATHER, SON, SPIRIT

Father, you are the Father of my Lord Jesus Christ. I bow my knees to you. From you every family in heaven and on earth is named. I praise you for the riches of your glory.

Through the good news, you give light to all men. You show us the unsearchable riches that are in Christ and your plan for all the ages, your eternal purpose that you accomplished through Christ.

For many generations the mystery of Christ was not made known to men, but you revealed it through your apostles and prophets in the Spirit.

It is this: that the Gentiles are fellow heirs and fellow members of the body, and fellow partakers of your promise in Christ Jesus.

Through us, the Church, you make known your wisdom to all the principalities and powers in the heavenly places.

Your might is glorious.

To you be the glory in the Church and in Christ Jesus to all generations forever and ever.

Father, there is one body, one Spirit, one hope of my calling, one Lord, one faith, one baptism, one God and Father of all. You are over all and through all and in all.

I have the consolation of your love, the fellowship of the Spirit, and your tender mercies and compassion.

Thank you that I am your child.

Thank you that in Christ you forgave me.

I sing and make melody in my heart to you.

I give you thanks for all things in the name of my Lord Jesus Christ!

EPHESIANS 3:4-6, 7-11, 14-16, 21; 4:4-6, 32; 5:19-20; PHILIPPIANS 2:1, 15; COLOSSIANS 1:11

CHRIST'S VICTORY

Father, thanks be to you! You always lead me in triumph in Christ.

Jesus, because you give me abundant grace and your gift of righteousness, I reign in life through you.

You died to sin once for all. I died with you. So I died to sin, too!

My old man was crucified with you, so my body of sin no longer holds power over me. I, who have died, am freed from sin!

Jesus, thank you that I can count on the fact that I died to sin, and am alive to God in you.

You have set me free from sin and made me a slave to righteousness. Sin doesn't rule over me, because I am not under law, but I am under your grace.

I praise you that now in my inner man I delight in your law. The law of sin still operates in the members of my body, but you deliver me from that!

Thank you that the law of your life-giving Spirit has set me free from the law of sin and death.

Father, I can't practice sin, because I am born of you, and your seed remains in me.

Jesus, you are my life. It is no longer I who live, but you live in me. The life you live, you live to God.

Holy Spirit, you dwell in me. My body is dead because of sin, but you are life in me because of righteousness. You give life to my mortal body.

Your mind is life and peace. I am led by you.

Jesus, it was for freedom that you set me free.

Father, Son, and Spirit, I praise you!

ROMANS 5:17; 6:2, 6-11, 14, 18, 22; 7:22-25; 8:2, 6, 9-11, 14;
2 CORINTHIANS 2:14; GALATIANS 2:20; 5:1, 18; 1 JOHN 3:9

Psalms

Lord, you have forgiven my iniquity.
> You have covered all my sin.

Mercy and truth meet together.
> Righteousness and peace have kissed each other.

Truth springs out of the earth.
> Righteousness has looked down from heaven.

Lord, you give me what is good.
> Righteousness goes before you,
> and prepares the way for your steps.

You, Lord, are good, and ready to forgive,
> abundant in lovingkindness to all those who call on you.

There is no one like you among the gods, Lord,
> nor any deeds like your deeds.

All nations you have made will come and worship before
> you, Lord.
> They will glorify your name.

For you are great, and you do wondrous things.
> You are God alone.

I will praise you, O Lord my God, with my whole heart.
> I will glorify your name forevermore.

For your lovingkindness is great toward me.
> You have delivered my soul from the lowest Sheol.

You are a merciful and gracious God,
> slow to anger, and abundant in lovingkindness and truth.

You are the God of my salvation.

You have been our dwelling place for all generations.
> Before the mountains were born,
> before you had formed the earth and the world,
> even from everlasting to everlasting, you are God.

For a thousand years in your sight are just like yesterday
> when it is past,
> like a watch in the night.

I praise you, Lord!

Psalm 85:2, 10-12; 86:5, 8-10, 12-13, 15; 88:1; 90:1-2, 4

THINGS TO COME

Jesus, you will appear a second time, without reference to sin, to us who eagerly wait for you for salvation.

You promised the crown of life to those who love you. Your coming is at hand.

Thank you that whatever good thing I do, I will receive the same good again from you.

Father, one day you will judge the living and the dead.

You have promised, "Yet once more I will shake not only the earth, but also the heavens."

You will remove those things that can be shaken, things that have been made, so those things which can't be shaken may remain.

Thank you that I receive a kingdom that can't be shaken.

Here I don't have a lasting city, but, like Abraham, I am seeking the city which is to come.

Abraham was an heir of your promise, and now I am, too. He considered you faithful who had made the promise.

He was looking for the city which has foundations. You are the architect and builder of that city. He desired a better country, a heavenly one.

That is my city, and my country, too. You are not ashamed to be called our God, for you have prepared that city for us.

I praise you!

EPHESIANS 6:8; HEBREWS 9:27; 11:9-11, 16; 12:27-28; JAMES 1:12; 5:8; 1 PETER 4:5

17TH SEVEN PRAISES

Praise the Lord!
Praise the Lord from the heavens!
Praise him in the heights!
Let them praise the name of the Lord,
for his name alone is exalted.
His glory is above the earth and the heavens.
Praise the Lord!

PSALM 148:1, 13-14

THE SOVEREIGN CREATOR OF ALL

Lord, who has measured the waters in the hollow of his hand,
    and marked off the sky with his span,
    and calculated the dust of the earth in a measuring basket,
    and weighed the mountains on scales,
    and the hills in a balance?
Who has directed your Spirit,
    or has taught you as your counselor?
Who did you take counsel with,
    and who instructed you,
    and taught you in the path of justice,
    and taught you knowledge,
    and showed you the way of understanding?
The nations are like a drop in a bucket,
    and are regarded as a speck of dust on a balance.
    You lift up the islands like fine dust.
All the nations are like nothing before you.
    They are regarded by you as less than nothing, and vanity.
To whom then will I liken you, Lord?
    Or what likeness will I compare to you?
Haven't I known?
    Haven't I heard?
    Wasn't I told from the beginning?
    Haven't I understood from the foundations of the earth?
It is you who sit above the circle of the earth,
    and its inhabitants are like grasshoppers;
    who stretch out the heavens like a curtain,
    and spread them out like a tent to dwell in.
Lord, you bring princes to nothing,
    and make the judges of the earth meaningless.
Scarcely are they planted,
    scarcely are they sown,
    their stock has scarcely taken root in the ground,
    but you merely blow on them, and they wither,
    and the whirlwind takes them away as stubble.
I praise you!

ISAIAH 40:12-15, 17-18, 21-24

PSALMS

I sing to you, Lord.
> I shout aloud to the rock of my salvation!
I come before your presence with thanksgiving
> and extol you with songs!
For you are a great God,
> a great King above all gods.
In your hand are the deep places of the earth.
> The heights of the mountains are also yours.
The sea is yours; you made it.
> Your hands formed the dry land.
I worship and bow down.
> I kneel before you, my Maker,
> for you are my God.
I am a sheep of your pasture,
> a sheep in your care.
I sing a new song to you, Lord,
> for you have done marvelous things!
> Your right hand and your holy arm have worked
> salvation for you.
You have made your salvation known.
> You have openly shown your righteousness in the sight
> of the nations.
You have remembered your lovingkindness and your
> faithfulness.
> All the ends of the earth have seen your salvation.
Make a joyful noise to the Lord, all the earth!
> Burst out and sing for joy, yes, sing praises!
I sing praises to you, Lord, with the voice of melody.
> With trumpets and the sound of the horn,
> make a joyful noise before the King, the Lord.
Let the sea roar with its fullness;
> the world, and those who dwell therein.
Let the rivers clap their hands.
> Let the mountains sing for joy together.
Let them sing before you, Lord,
> for you come to judge the earth.
You will judge the world with righteousness,
> and the peoples with equity.

PSALM 85:1-7; 98:1-9

THE LOVING AND FAITHFUL GOD

Jesus, the Lord formed you from the womb to be his Servant,
  to bring Jacob again to him,
  and to gather Israel to him.
You were honored in the Lord's eyes;
  God was your strength.
You were his Servant, to raise up the tribes of Jacob,
  and to restore the preserved of Israel.
He gave you as a light to the nations,
  that you would be his salvation to the end of the earth.
You were the despised One, whom the nation abhorred.
  You were the Servant of rulers.
The Lord God, the Redeemer of Israel, the Holy One, said to you:

  "Kings shall see and rise up,
  princes, and they shall worship,
  because I, who am faithful,
  even the Holy One of Israel, have chosen you.
  I have answered you in an acceptable time.
  I have helped you in a day of salvation.
  I will preserve you and give you for a covenant
    of the people."

Jesus, you were not rebellious.
  You did not turn back.
You gave your back to those who beat you,
  and your cheeks to those who pluck out the beard.
  You didn't hide your face from shame and spitting.
The Lord God helped you,
  so you were not disgraced.
Therefore you set your face like a flint,
  and knew you would not be disappointed.
Lord, how beautiful on the mountains are the feet of him
    who brings good news,
  who announces peace, who brings good news of
    happiness,
  who proclaims salvation, who says, "Your God reigns!"
I praise you, Lord!

ISAIAH 49:5-8; 50:4-7; 52:7

Father, Son, Spirit

Jesus, you came not to judge the world, but to save the world.

As the Father raises the dead and gives them life, so you give life to whom you desire.

As Moses lifted up the serpent in the wilderness, even so you had to be lifted up, that whoever believes in you should not perish, but have eternal life.

The Father judges no one. He gave all judgment to you, that all may honor you, even as they honor the Father. Whoever doesn't honor you doesn't honor the Father who sent you.

Jesus, you have the words of eternal life.

The words that you speak to us are spirit, and they are life.

You are the shepherd of the sheep. The sheep listen to your voice. You call your sheep by name, and you lead us out. You go before us, and we follow you. We know your voice.

You know your own, and we know you, just as the Father knows you, and you know the Father.

We sheep hear your voice, Jesus, and you know us, and we follow you. You give eternal life to us. We will never perish, and no one will snatch us out of your hand.

Father, you gave us to Jesus. You are greater than all. No one is able to snatch us out of your hand.

Jesus, you and the Father are one.

Your kingdom is not of this world.

In you I have peace. I will have trouble in the world, but I have joy, because you have overcome the world.

Because of you, my heart rejoices, and no one will take my joy away from me.

John 3:14-15; 5:21-23; 6:63, 68; 10:1-4, 14-15, 27-30; 12:47; 16:22, 33; 18:36

CHRIST'S VICTORY

Father, thank you for your law. It is holy and righteous and good. Through it I came to know my sin. It was my tutor to lead me to Christ, so I could be made right with you by faith.

And thank you, Father, that now that faith has come, I am no longer under a tutor!

Instead, I am your son through faith in Christ. I have been baptized into him.

I praise you, Jesus, that I have been crucified with you. I died to the law through your body. I've been released from the law.

I died to what bound me, so I might be joined to you instead, so I could bear fruit for God.

I praise you that you are the end of the law for righteousness to everyone who believes.

Jesus, the law could never give me life. I praise you that you are the life!

It is no longer I who live, but you live in me.

I live by faith in you.

The law aroused sinful passions and bore fruit for death. The law was the power of sin. It was the ministry of death and condemnation.

Holy Spirit, I praise you that though the letter kills, you give life!

If the ministry of death through Moses had glory, how will your ministry of life not be even more glorious!

You are the Spirit of life. You, who live in me, give life to my mortal body.

Holy Spirit, you are the Lord. Where you are, there is liberty. As in a mirror, I see and reflect the Lord's glory. You are transforming me into the same image, from glory to glory.

Holy Spirit, I praise you!

JOHN 14:6; ROMANS 3:20; 7:4-6, 12; 8:2, 11; 10:4; 1 CORINTHIANS 15:56; 2 CORINTHIANS 3:6-10, 17-18; GALATIANS 2:19-20; 3:21, 24-27

PSALMS

I will sing of your lovingkindness forever, Lord.
 With my mouth, I will make known your faithfulness
  to all generations.
I will declare, "Love stands firm forever.
 You established the heavens.
 Your faithfulness is in them."
You made a covenant with your chosen one.
 You swore to David, your servant,
That you would establish his offspring forever,
 and establish his throne to all generations.
The heavens will praise your wonders, Lord,
 your faithfulness in the assembly of the holy ones.
For who in the heavens can be compared to you?
 Who among the sons of the heavenly beings is like you,
A very awesome God in the council of the holy ones,
 to be feared above all those around you?
Lord, God of hosts, who is a mighty one like you?
 Your faithfulness surrounds you.
You rule the pride of the sea.
 When its waves rise up, you calm them.
You have scattered your enemies with your mighty arm.
The heavens are yours.
 The earth also is yours,
 the world and its fullness.
 You have founded them.
You have created the north and the south.
 Tabor and Hermon rejoice in your name.
You have a mighty arm.
 Your hand is strong, and your right hand is exalted.
Righteousness and justice are the foundation of your throne.
 Lovingkindness and truth go before your face.

I praise you, Lord!

PSALM 89:1-14

THINGS TO COME

I praise you, God, the Father of my Lord Jesus Christ.

According to your great mercy, you caused me to be born again to a living hope through the resurrection of Jesus Christ from the dead.

You have given me an incorruptible and undefiled inheritance that won't fade away, reserved in heaven for me.

By your power I am guarded through faith for a salvation ready to be revealed in the last time.

Father, I greatly rejoice in these things.

I know that the proof of my faith, which is more precious than perishable gold, will be found to result in praise, glory, and honor at the revelation of Jesus Christ.

Jesus, though I haven't seen you, I love you. Though I don't see you now, I believe in you, and so I rejoice greatly with joy that is unspeakable and full of glory.

I know that I will receive the result of my faith, the salvation of my soul.

I set my hope fully on the grace that will be brought to me at your revelation.

Jesus, because of your suffering I will share in the glory that will be revealed. When you, the chief Shepherd, are revealed, I will receive the crown of glory that doesn't fade away.

All my praise goes to you!

1 PETER 1:3-13; 5:1-4

18th Seven Praises

Sing to the Lord a new song,
and his praise from the end of the earth.
Let them shout from the top of the mountains!
Let them give glory to the Lord,
and declare his praise.

Isaiah 42:10-12

THE SOVEREIGN CREATOR OF ALL

To whom will I liken you, Lord?
    Who is your equal?
I lift up my eyes to the heavens,
    and see who has created the stars.
You bring out their army by number.
    You call them all by name.
    By the greatness of your might,
    because of the strength of your power,
    not one of them is missing.

Haven't I known?
    Haven't I heard?
The everlasting God, the Lord,
    the Creator of the ends of the earth, doesn't faint.
    You don't grow weary.
    Your understanding is unsearchable.
You give power to the weak.
    You increase the strength of him who has no might.
Even the youths faint and get weary,
    and the young men utterly fall;
But I, who wait for you, will renew my strength.
    I will mount up with wings like an eagle.
    I will run, and not be weary.
    I will walk, and not faint.

Lord, you have declared the former things from of old.
    They went out of your mouth, and you revealed them.
    You did them suddenly, and they happened.
You declared it to us from of old;
    before it came to pass you showed it to us.
For your own sake,
    for your own sake, you will do it;
You will not give your glory to another.

I stand in awe of you, O Holy One!

ISAIAH 29:23; 40:25-31; 48:3, 5, 11

Psalms

Blessed are the people who learn to acclaim you, Lord.
> They walk in the light of your presence.
In your name they rejoice all day.
> In your righteousness, they are exalted.
For you are the glory of their strength.
> In your favor, my horn will be exalted.
For my shield belongs to you, Lord, to the Holy One.
> Your faithfulness and lovingkindness will be with me.
You are my Father, my God, and the rock of my salvation!
Lord, your covenant will stand firm with David.
> You will make his offspring endure forever,
> and his throne as the days of heaven.
You will not break your covenant,
> nor alter what your lips have uttered.
You have sworn by your holiness,

> "I will not lie to David.
> His offspring will endure forever,
> his throne like the sun before me.
> It will be established forever like the moon,
> the faithful witness in the sky."

Lord, blessed be you forevermore!

You are the God to whom vengeance belongs.
> You know the thoughts of man, that they are futile.
You won't reject your people,
> neither will you forsake your inheritance.
Lord, you have been my help.
> When I said, "My foot is slipping!"
> Your lovingkindness, Lord, held me up.
In the multitude of my anxious thoughts,
> your comforts delight my soul.
You have been my high tower,
> my God, the rock of my refuge.

Psalm 89:15-18, 24, 26, 28-29, 34-37, 52; 94:1, 11-12, 17-19, 22

THE LOVING AND FAITHFUL GOD

Sing, O heavens, and be joyful, O earth!
  Break out into singing, mountains,
For you comfort your people, Lord,
  and have compassion on your afflicted.
Lord, you have not forsaken me,
  or forgotten me.
Can a woman forget her nursing child,
  that she should not have compassion on the son
    of her womb?
Even if she may forget,
   yet you will not forget me!
You have engraved me on the palms of your hands.
  I am continually before you.

You are the Lord my God; you will help me.
  Who is he who will condemn me?
  I will revere you, Lord.
The one who walks in darkness and has no light,
  let him trust in your name, Lord, and rely on his God.

Lord, I look to Abraham,
  who was but one man when you called him.
   You blessed him and made him many.
Lord, you comfort me.
  You make the wilderness like Eden,
  and the desert like the garden of the Lord.
Joy and gladness will be mine,
  thanksgiving, and the voice of melody.
Everlasting joy shall be on my head.
  I will obtain gladness and joy.
  Sorrow and sighing will flee away.

Lord, you are my confidence.
  Whoever trusts in you is blessed.
Every word of yours is flawless.
  You are a shield to those who take refuge in you.

ISAIAH 49:13-16, 23, 26; 50:9-10; 51:2-3, 11; PROVERBS 3:26; 16:20; 30:5

Father, Son, Spirit

Holy Spirit, when God's kindness and love toward me appeared, he saved me by your washing and your regeneration.

I was washed, and sanctified, and justified in the name of the Lord Jesus, and in you.

When I first heard the word of truth, and believed, you sealed me in Christ for the day of my redemption.

You are the down payment that the Father has given me in my heart. You are the pledge of my inheritance until I, God's possession, am fully redeemed—all to the praise of his glory.

My body is your temple. You are in me. You are life in me.

In you, Holy Spirit, I have access to the Father.

I worship God in you.

Through you the love of God has been poured into my heart.

Through you I wait by faith for the hope of righteousness.

Through you the Father strengthens me with power in my inner person, that Christ may dwell in my heart through faith.

Through you the Father roots me in love, and strengthens me to know how wide and long and high and deep his love is, so that I can know his love which surpasses knowledge, and be filled with all of God's fullness.

Holy Spirit, those who are in the flesh can't please God. But I am no longer in the flesh. I am in you! You dwell in me.

Holy Spirit, I praise you!

Romans 5:5; 8:8-10; 1 Corinthians 6:11, 19; 12:3; 2 Corinthians 1:22; Galatians 5:5; Ephesians 1:13-14; 2:18; 3:16-19; 4:30; Philippians 3:3; Titus 3:3-5

CHRIST'S VICTORY

Jesus, by grace you saved me through faith. I received you by believing in you.

I praise you that in the same way I received you, now I walk in you.

Holy Spirit, I didn't receive you by keeping the law. I received you by hearing with faith. I began with you! I can't be completed by my own human effort.

I walk by faith, not by sight. The righteous live by faith.

Your righteousness is revealed through the good news from faith to faith.

Jesus, the life that I now live, I live by faith in you. It is no longer I who live. You live in me.

Of your fullness I have received, and grace upon grace.

Father, you are the God of all grace. You called me to your eternal glory in Christ. You perfect, confirm, strengthen, and establish me. By your grace I am what I am.

I praise you that I am an heir of the grace of life. My heart is established by grace. I am strengthened by your grace. The word of your grace builds me up.

I praise you that I can draw near with boldness to the throne of grace, that I may receive mercy and may find grace for help in time of need.

I praise you for the glory of your grace!

JOHN 1:12-13, 16; ACTS 20:32; ROMANS 1:16-17; 1 CORINTHIANS 15:9; 2 CORINTHIANS 5:7; 9:14; GALATIANS 2:20; 3:2-5; EPHESIANS 1:6; 2:8; COLOSSIANS 2:6; 2 TIMOTHY 2:1; HEBREWS 4:16; 13:9; 1 PETER 3:7; 5:10

Psalms

Lord, he who dwells in the secret place of the Most High
     will rest in the shadow of the Almighty.
I will say of you, "You are my refuge and my fortress;
     my God, in whom I trust."
You will deliver me from the snare of the fowler,
     and from the deadly pestilence.
You will cover me with your feathers.
     Under your wings I will take refuge.
     Your faithfulness is my shield and rampart.
I will not be afraid of the terror by night,
     nor of the arrow that flies by day,
     nor of the pestilence that walks in darkness,
     nor of the destruction that wastes at noonday.
A thousand may fall at my side,
     and ten thousand at my right hand;
     but it will not come near me.
I will only look with my eyes,
     and see the recompense of the wicked.
Because I have made you my refuge, Lord,
     the Most High my dwelling place,
No evil will happen to me,
     neither shall any plague come near my dwelling.
For you will put your angels in charge of me,
     to guard me in all my ways.
They will bear me up in their hands,
     so that I won't dash my foot against a stone.
I will tread on the lion and cobra.
     I will trample the young lion and the serpent underfoot.
Because I have set my love on you, Lord,
     therefore you will deliver me.
     You will set me on high, because you have known my name.
I will call on you, Lord, and you will answer me.
     You will be with me in trouble.
     You will deliver me, and honor me.
You will satisfy me with long life,
     and show me your salvation.

Psalm 91:1-16

THINGS TO COME

Lord, with you one day is as a thousand years, and a thousand years as one day.

You are not slow concerning your promise, but you are patient, not wishing that anyone should perish, but that all should come to repentance.

Your day, Jesus, will come as a thief in the night. The heavens will pass away with a roar, and the elements will be dissolved with intense heat, and the earth and the works that are in it will be burned up. In this way all these things will be destroyed.

Lord, I look for and earnestly desire the coming of the day of God, which will cause the burning heavens to be dissolved, and the elements to melt with intense heat.

By your word the heavens that exist now and the earth are being reserved for fire, being kept against the day of judgment and destruction of ungodly men.

According to your promise, I await a new heavens and a new earth, in which righteousness dwells.

Jesus, to you be the glory, both now and to the day of eternity!

You will come with ten thousands of your holy ones, to execute judgment on all, and to convict all the ungodly of all their works of ungodliness which they have done in an ungodly way, and of all the harsh things which ungodly sinners have spoken against you.

But Lord Jesus, I stay in your love and look for your mercy that brings eternal life.

You are able to keep me from stumbling, and to present me blameless before the presence of your glory in great joy— to you, God, my Savior, who alone are wise, be glory and majesty, dominion and power, both now and forever.

2 PETER 3:7-13, 18; JUDE 1:4, 6-7, 13-15, 21-25

19TH SEVEN PRAISES

I will always praise you.
My mouth will be filled with your praise,
with your honor all day long.
I will continually hope
and will praise you more and more.
My lips will shout for joy!
My soul, which you have redeemed,
sings praises to you!

PSALM 71:6, 8, 14, 23

THE SOVEREIGN CREATOR OF ALL

Lord, I sing to you a new song.
Your praise will be from the end of the earth,
    from those who go down to the sea,
    and all that is therein,
    the islands and their inhabitants.
Let the wilderness and its cities raise their voices,
    let them shout from the top of the mountains!
Let them give glory to you, Lord,
    and declare your praise in the islands.
You will go out like a warrior.
    You will stir up zeal like a man of war.
    You will raise a war cry.
    Yes, you will shout aloud.
    You will triumph over your enemies.
You will destroy mountains and hills,
    and dry up all their vegetation.
You will make the rivers islands,
    and will dry up the pools.
You will bring the blind by a way that they don't know.
    You will make darkness light before them,
    and crooked places straight.
You will do these things,
    and you will not forsake them.

Lord, we have arisen and we shine, for your light has come,
    and your glory has risen.
Darkness covers the earth,
    and thick darkness the peoples;
But you have arisen on us,
    and your glory is seen on us.
Nations come to your light,
    and kings to the brightness of your rising.

I praise you, Lord!

ISAIAH 42:10-13, 15-17; 60:1-3

Psalms

It is good to give you thanks, Lord,
    to sing praises to your name, Most High,
To proclaim your lovingkindness in the morning,
    and your faithfulness every night.
For you, Lord, have made me glad by what you have done.
    I will rejoice in the works of your hands.
How great are your works, Lord!
    Your thoughts are very deep.
You are on high forevermore.
Your enemies will perish.
    All the evildoers will be scattered.
But you have exalted my horn.
    I am anointed with fresh oil.
You are my rock,
    and there is no unrighteousness in you.

Lord, you reign!
    You are clothed with majesty!
    You are armed with strength.
The world also is established;
    it can't be moved.
Your throne is established from long ago.
    You are from everlasting.
The floods have lifted up, Lord,
    the floods have lifted up their voice.
    The floods lift up their waves.
Above the voices of many waters,
    the mighty breakers of the sea,
    you are mighty on high.
Your statutes stand firm.
    Holiness adorns your house,
    Lord, forevermore.

I praise you, Lord!

Psalm 92:1-2, 4-5, 8-10, 15; 93:1-5

THE LOVING AND FAITHFUL GOD

Father, you have performed the good word which you spoke concerning the house of Israel and the house of Judah. You have caused a Branch of righteousness to be raised up to David. He will execute justice and righteousness.

Jesus, you were the Father's servant.
    You were exalted and lifted up very high.
People were astonished at you—
        your appearance was marred more than any man,
        your form so disfigured you no longer looked human.
        But you cleansed many nations.
Kings will be astounded at your exaltation;
        they will see what has not been told them,
        and they will understand what they had not heard.
        Through you God's arm has been revealed.
You grew up before the Father as a tender plant,
        and as a root out of dry ground.
You had no good looks or majesty.
        When people looked at you, you had no beauty that
            we should desire you.
You were despised
        and rejected by men,
A man of suffering
        and acquainted with grief.
You were despised, as one from whom men hide their face;
        and we didn't regard you.
You bore my sickness
        and carried my suffering;
Yet I considered you smitten,
        struck by God, and afflicted.
You were pierced for my transgressions.
        You were crushed for my iniquities.
The punishment that brought me peace was on you;
        and by your wounds I am healed.

ISAIAH 52:13-15; 53:1-5; JEREMIAH 33:14-15

FATHER, SON, SPIRIT

Father, you are my Savior, the Father of my Lord Jesus Christ. I am loved by you.

You chose me from the beginning for salvation through the Spirit's sanctification and belief in the truth. You called me through the good news, so I could obtain the glory of my Lord Jesus Christ.

You are the blessed God. The good news is the news of your glory.

You are the King eternal, immortal, invisible. You alone are wise. To you be honor and glory forever and ever.

God, you are my Savior. You want all people to be saved and come to a full knowledge of the truth.

There is one God, and one mediator between God and men, the man Christ Jesus. He gave himself as a ransom for all.

You are the living and true God. I have set my trust in you. You are the Savior of all men, especially of those who believe.

You give life to all things. You richly provide me with everything to enjoy.

You are the blessed and only Ruler, the King of kings, and Lord of lords.

You alone have immortality, dwelling in unapproachable light, whom no man has seen, nor can see. To you be honor and eternal power.

You didn't give me a spirit of fear, but of power, love, and self-control.

Father, you cannot lie. You promised us eternal life before time began.

I praise you!

1 THESSALONIANS 1:9; 2 THESSALONIANS 2:13-14; 1 TIMOTHY 1:1, 11, 17; 2:4; 4:11; 6:13, 15-17; 2 TIMOTHY 1:7; TITUS 1:2

CHRIST'S VICTORY

Jesus, you are Lord of all. God anointed you with the Holy Spirit and with power. You went about doing good and healing all who were oppressed by the devil.

You appeared on earth to destroy the works of the devil.

You became flesh and blood like me, so through death you might bring to nothing the devil, who had the power of death.

Father, when Jesus went to the cross, the prince of this world was cast out. At the cross, you disarmed the rulers and powers. You made an open display of them, triumphing over them through Christ.

By the strength of your might, you raised Jesus from the dead and sat him at your right hand in the heavenly places.

Jesus, you are seated in the heavenlies, far above all rule, authority, power, dominion, and every name that is named, not only in this age, but also in that which is to come. The Father made all things subject to you, under your feet, and made you head over all things for us, the Church.

This was your eternal purpose, Father. Now, through the Church, your wisdom is made known to the principalities and powers in the heavenly places.

Father, you delivered me from the domain of darkness, and translated me into the kingdom of the Son of your love.

I am born of you. I am of you. The whole world lies in the power of the evil one, but because I am born of you, you keep me, and the evil one does not touch me.

Jesus, you are faithful. You establish me and guard me from the evil one.

Holy Spirit, I am of God, and have overcome them, because greater are you who are in me than he who is in the world.

I praise you, Father, Son, and Spirit!

JOHN 12:31; 17:15; ACTS 10:36, 38; 2 CORINTHIANS 2:14; EPHESIANS 1:20-23; 3:10-11; COLOSSIANS 1:13; 2:15; 2 THESSALONIANS 3:3-4; HEBREWS 2:14; 1 JOHN 3:8; 4:4; 5:18-20

PSALMS

Lord, I sing to you a new song!
    Sing to the Lord, all the earth.
I sing to you, Lord, I bless your name;
    I proclaim your salvation from day to day.
I declare your glory among the nations,
    your marvelous works among all the peoples.
For you are great and greatly to be praised;
    you are to be feared above all gods.
For all the gods of the peoples are idols,
    but you made the heavens.
Honor and majesty are before you;
    strength and beauty are in your sanctuary.
Ascribe to the Lord, you families of nations,
    ascribe to him glory and strength.
I ascribe to you the glory due your name, Lord;
    I worship you in the beauty of your holiness!
Tremble before him, all the earth.
    Say among the nations, "The Lord reigns."
The world is established,
    it can't be moved;
    you will judge the peoples righteously.
Let the heavens be glad, and let the earth rejoice;
    let the sea roar, and all its fullness;
    let the field and all that is in it exult.
Then all the trees of the woods will sing for joy
      before you, Lord.
For you are coming,
    you are coming to judge the earth.
You will judge the world with righteousness,
    the peoples with your truth.

Lord, you are righteous.
    Your judgments are upright.
Your righteousness is an everlasting righteousness.

I praise you, Lord!

PSALM 96:1-13; 119:137, 142

THINGS TO COME

Father, you are, and you have been, and you are to come. You are the Alpha and the Omega, who is and who was and who is to come, the Almighty.

Jesus, when John saw you, you were like a son of man, clothed with a robe reaching down to your feet, with a golden sash around your chest.

Your head and your hair were white as white wool, like snow.

Your eyes were like a flame of fire.

Your feet were like burnished bronze, as if it had been refined in a furnace.

Your voice was like the voice of many waters.

You had seven stars in your right hand.

Out of your mouth came a sharp two-edged sword.

Your face was like the sun shining at its brightest.

John fell at your feet as a dead man, but you placed your right hand on him and said, "Don't be afraid."

You are the first and the last, and the Living One. You were dead, and behold, you are alive forever and ever.

You have the keys of Death and of Hades.

I praise you!

REVELATION 1:4, 8, 13-18

20th Seven Praises

Make a joyful shout to God, all the earth!
Sing to the glory of his name!
Offer glory and praise!
Tell God, "How awesome are your deeds!
All the earth will worship you,
and will sing to you;
they will sing to your name."

PSALM 66:1-2, 4

THE SOVEREIGN CREATOR OF ALL

Lord, you are one who made me.
>You formed me from the womb.
>You have chosen me.
You pour water on him who is thirsty,
>and streams on the dry ground.
You have poured your Spirit on your people,
>your blessing on us.
Lord, I am yours.
You are my King.
>You are my Redeemer, the Lord of hosts.
You are the first, and you are the last;
>besides you there is no God.
Who is like you?
>Who will call,
>and will declare it,
>and set all things in order, but you?
No one but you can declare the things that are coming,
>and have them happen.
I will not fear, or be afraid.
>You declared it long ago and have shown it.
>I am your witness.
There is no God besides you.
>There is no other Rock.

Lord, you are God, and there is no one else.
>Besides you, there is no God.
From the rising of the sun to its setting,
>there is no one besides you.
You are God, and there is no one else.
>You form the light and create darkness.
>You make peace and create calamity.
You are God, who does all these things.

I praise you!

Is 44:2-3, 5-8; 45:5-7

PSALMS

Lord, you reign!
>Let the earth rejoice!
>Let the multitude of islands be glad!

Clouds and darkness are around you.
>Righteousness and justice are the foundation of
>>your throne.

A fire goes before you,
>and burns up your adversaries on every side.

Your lightning lights up the world.
>The earth sees, and trembles.

The mountains melt like wax at your presence,
>at the presence of the Lord of the whole earth.

The heavens declare your righteousness.
>All the peoples have seen your glory.

For you, Lord, are most high above all the earth.
>You are exalted far above all gods.

You preserve the souls of your saints.
>You deliver them out of the hand of the wicked.

You sow light for the righteous,
>and gladness for the upright in heart.

Be glad in the Lord, you righteous!
>I give thanks to your holy name.

Shout for joy to the Lord, all the earth!
>Serve him with gladness.
>I come before your presence, Lord, with singing.

I know that you are God.
>It is you who have made me, and I am yours.
>We are your people, and the sheep of your pasture.

I enter into your gates with thanksgiving,
>and into your courts with praise.
>I give thanks to you, and bless your name.

For you are good, Lord.
>Your lovingkindness endures forever,
>your faithfulness to all generations.

PSALM 97:1-6, 9-12; 100:1-5

THE LOVING AND FAITHFUL GOD

Jesus, all we like sheep have gone astray.
    Everyone has turned to his own way;
    God laid on you the iniquity of us all.
You were oppressed,
    yet when you were afflicted you didn't open your mouth.
As a lamb that is led to the slaughter,
    and as a sheep that before its shearers is silent,
    so you didn't open your mouth.
You were taken away by oppression and judgment.
    As for your generation,
    who cared that you were cut off from among the living?
    You were stricken for my disobedience.
They made your grave with the wicked,
    and with a rich man in your death,
Although you had done no violence,
    nor was any deceit in your mouth.
Yet it pleased God to bruise you,
    putting you to grief.
    He made your soul an offering for sin.
So you have seen your offspring;
    God has prolonged your days;
    the will of God has prospered in your hand.
After the suffering of your soul,
    you saw light and were satisfied.
You, the Father's righteous Servant, have justified the many;
    you have borne our iniquities.
Therefore God has given you a portion with the great.
    You have divided the plunder with the strong,
Because you poured out your soul to death
    and were counted with the transgressors;
Yet you bore the sins of many
    and made intercession for the transgressors.

Lord Jesus, I praise you!

ISAIAH 53:6-12

Father, Son, Spirit

Jesus, the Father made you both Lord and Christ. You are the stone which was regarded as worthless, which has become the head of the corner.

God did mighty works and wonders and signs by you.

The Father promised not to allow you, the Holy One, to undergo decay, and you didn't. When God raised you from the dead, he fulfilled the good news of the promise that he made to his people.

There is salvation in no one else but you, for there is no other name under heaven by which we must be saved.

Father, you had Jesus put to death through his being hung on a cross. But you raised him. You exalted him to your right hand as a Prince and a Savior, to grant repentance and forgiveness of sins.

Lord Jesus, you are the Righteous One. You are the Son of Man, at the right hand of God. May your name be magnified!

Stephen saw the heavens opened. He saw the glory of God and you standing at the right hand of God.

Jesus, you are the Son of God. You are Lord of all. Peace comes through you.

The prophets and Moses said what was going to take place, that you were to suffer, and that by reason of your resurrection from the dead you would be the first to proclaim light both to Jews and Gentiles.

Through you is the forgiveness of sins.

By you everyone who believes is freed from all things that the law of Moses couldn't free them from.

I praise you that I am saved through your grace, Lord Jesus!

Acts 2:22, 36; 4:10-12; 5:30-31; 7:52, 55-56; 9:20; 10:36; 13:32-39; 15:11; 17:3; 19:17; 22:14; 26:22-23

CHRIST'S VICTORY

Father, from you, and through you, and to you are all things.

You are the one God and Father of all. You are over all and through all and in all.

In all of your wisdom and insight, you made known to us the mystery of your will. You did this according to the plan you established in Christ. You will bring it to pass when the time is right.

Your plan is this: that all things would be summed up in Christ—both things in the heavens and things on the earth—and that he would have the supremacy in everything.

Father, you work all things according to the council of your will. Your purpose is unchangeable.

You are bringing many children to glory. You work all things in all.

You predestined me for this according to your purpose and gave me an inheritance in Christ. So I am a praise to the glory of your grace—I who have hoped in Christ.

You cause all things to work together for good to me. You predestined me to be conformed to the image of your Son.

What you began in me, you will finish.

So I give you thanks for all things in the name of my Lord Jesus Christ.

You called me according to your purpose. You predestined me, and called me, and justified me, and glorified me.

From you, Father, are all things, and through you are all things. To you be the glory in the Church and in Christ Jesus to all generations forever and ever!

Jesus, to you belong the glory and the dominion forever and ever!

ROMANS 8:28-30; 11:36; 1 CORINTHIANS 8:6; 12:6; EPHESIANS 1:8-12; 3:21; 4:4-6; 5:20; PHILIPPIANS 1:6; COLOSSIANS 1:18; HEBREWS 2:10; 6:17; 1 PETER 4:11

PSALMS

Lord, you reign! Let the peoples tremble.
> You sit enthroned among the cherubim.
> Let the earth be moved.
You are great, Lord.
> You are high above all the peoples.
I praise your great and awesome name.
> You are holy!
> You are my strength.
You love justice.
> You establish equity.
> You execute justice and righteousness.
I exalt you, O Lord my God.
> I worship at your footstool.
> You are holy!
I exalt you, O Lord my God.
> I worship you,
> for you are holy!

You, Lord, remain forever;
> your fame endures to all generations.
The nations will fear your name,
> all the kings of the earth your glory.
For you have built up Zion.
> You have appeared in your glory.
A people you are creating will praise you, Lord.
> Your years are throughout all generations.
Of old, you laid the foundation of the earth.
> The heavens are the work of your hands.
They will perish, but you will endure.
> All of them will wear out like a garment.
> You will change them like a cloak, and they will
> > be changed.
But you are the same.
> Your years will have no end.

PSALM 99:1-5, 9; 102:12, 15-18, 24-27

THINGS TO COME

Jesus, you are the faithful witness, the firstborn of the dead, and the ruler of the kings of the earth.

You loved me, and washed me from my sins by your blood. You made me to be part of your kingdom, a priest to your God and Father.

To you be the glory and the dominion forever and ever!

You are coming with the clouds, and every eye will see you, including those who pierced you. All the tribes of the earth will mourn over you.

Jesus, you walk among the seven golden lampstands. You are the first and the last. You were dead, and have come to life.

You have the sharp two-edged sword. You are the Son of God. Your eyes are like a flame of fire, and your feet are like burnished brass.

You are he who searches the hearts and the minds.

You have the seven Spirits of God and the seven stars. You are holy. You are true.

You have the key of David. You open and no one can shut; you shut and no one opens.

You are the Amen, the Faithful and True Witness, the Originator of God's creation.

You have loved me.

You are coming quickly, Jesus!

REVELATION 1:5-7; 2:1, 8, 18, 23; 3:1, 7, 9, 11, 14, 21

21st Seven Praises

Oh give thanks to the Lord.
Call on his name.
Make what he has done known among the peoples!
Sing to him.
Sing praises to him.
Tell of all his wondrous works!
Glory in his holy name.

1 Chronicles 16:8-10

The Sovereign Creator of All

Lord, let the heavens pour down righteousness,
    and the earth bring forth salvation.
God, you have created it.
    You are my Father.
    I am the clay and you are the potter.
    I am the work of your hand.
How could I strive with you, my Maker?
    I am a clay pot among the clay pots of the earth.
Shall the clay ask him who fashions it, "What are you making?"
    Woe to the one who says to a father, "What have you
        become the father of?"
    or to a mother, "What have you given birth to?"
Lord, you are my Maker, the Holy One.
    I ask you about the things to come,
    and commit to you the work of your hands.
You made the earth and created man on it.
    You, even your hands, have stretched out the heavens.
    You have commanded all their host.
You have raised me up in righteousness;
    you will make all my ways straight.
You are God and there is no one else.
    There is no other god.
You are a God who has hidden yourself,
    the God of Israel, the Savior.
You will save with an everlasting salvation.
    Never in all eternity will I be disappointed.
For you created the heavens;
    you formed the earth and made it;
    you established it and formed it to be inhabited.
By wisdom, Lord, you founded the earth.
    By understanding, you established the heavens.
Wisdom was yours, Lord, in the beginning of your work,
    before your deeds of old.
It was set up from everlasting, from the beginning,
    before the earth existed.
You are the I AM. There is no other.

Proverbs 3:19; 8:22-23; Isaiah 45:8-18; 64:8

Psalms

I will sing of lovingkindness and justice.
>To you, Lord, I will sing praises.

Your lovingkindness comes to me,
>your salvation, according to your word.
You are my portion.

I give thanks to you, Lord! I call on your name!
>I make your deeds known among the peoples.
I sing to you, I sing praises to you!
>I tell of all your marvelous works.
I glory in your holy name.
>Let the heart of those who seek you rejoice.
I seek you and your strength.
>I seek your face forevermore.
I remember your marvelous works that you have done:
>your wonders, and the judgments of your mouth.
You are the Lord, my God.
>Your judgments are in all the earth.
You have remembered your covenant forever,
>the word which you commanded to a thousand
>>generations,
The covenant which you made with Abraham,
>an everlasting covenant.
I praise you, Lord!

I praise you, Lord!
>I give thanks to you, for you are good.
>Your lovingkindness endures forever.
Who can utter your mighty acts,
>or fully declare all your praise?
Blessed be you, Lord,
>from everlasting even to everlasting!
I praise you, Lord!

Psalm 101:1; 105:1-9, 45; 106:1-2, 48; 119:41, 57

THE LOVING AND FAITHFUL GOD

Lord, you are our Maker, and our Husband.
    The Lord of hosts is your name.
The Holy One is my Redeemer.
    You are the God of the whole earth.
You have gathered us with great mercies;
    with everlasting lovingkindness
    you have had mercy on me.
The mountains may depart,
    and the hills be removed;
But your lovingkindness will not depart from me,
    and your covenant of peace will not be removed.

Lord, you say,

    "Come, everyone who thirsts, to the waters!
    Come, you who have no money, buy, and eat!
    Yes, come, buy wine and milk without money and
        without price.
    Eat that which is good,
    and let your soul delight itself in richness."

Lord, you have made an everlasting covenant,
    according to your mercy.
You are the Lord my God, the Holy One;
    you have glorified me.
    You have had mercy on me, and freely pardoned.
For your thoughts are not my thoughts,
    and your ways are not my ways.
For as the heavens are higher than the earth,
    so are your ways higher than my ways,
    and your thoughts than my thoughts.

Lord, you are the high and lofty One.
    You inhabit eternity.
    Your name is Holy.
    You dwell in the high and holy place.
You say, "Peace, peace, to him who is far off and to him
        who is near,
    and I will heal him."

ISAIAH 54:5-10; 55:1-9; 57:15, 19

Father, Son, Spirit

Father, you are the living God. You are the builder of all things. You are the Father of spirits.

By faith I understand that the universe was prepared by your word, so that what is seen was not made out of things which are visible.

From you are all things, and through you are all things. You are bringing many children to glory.

You have made me holy, a partaker of your heavenly calling. You have made me a partaker of Christ.

I have come to Mount Zion, to your city, the city of the living God, the heavenly Jerusalem, to innumerable angels, to the general assembly of the firstborn who are enrolled in heaven.

I have come to you, the Judge of all, and to the spirits of righteous men made perfect. And I have come to Jesus, the mediator of a new covenant.

You yourself said, "I will never leave you, nor will I ever forsake you." You are my helper. I will not fear. What can man do to me?

Father, you are the God of peace. You brought from the dead the great Shepherd of the sheep in the blood of the eternal covenant, my Lord Jesus.

You are able to equip me in every good work to do your will, working in me that which is well pleasing in your sight, through Jesus Christ.

To him be the glory forever and ever!

Hebrews 2:10; 3:1, 4, 12, 14; 11:3, 31; 12:9, 22-24; 13:5-6, 20-21

CHRIST'S VICTORY

Father, you have blessed me with every spiritual blessing in the heavenlies in Christ.

Your divine power has granted me all things pertaining to life and godliness. These come through knowing you.

You called me by your own glory and excellence, and have given me your precious and exceedingly great promises. Through these I become a partaker of the divine nature!

Jesus, you are the power of God and the wisdom of God. I am in you by the Father's doing. You were made to me wisdom from God, and righteousness, and sanctification, and redemption.

You are the bread of life, Jesus. I who have come to you will not be hungry, and I who believe in you will never be thirsty.

I drink the water you give, and I will never thirst again. The water you give me becomes in me a well of water springing up to eternal life.

I have believed in you, and from within me flow rivers of living water, the Holy Spirit.

Jesus, your grace is sufficient for me, for your power is made perfect in weakness. So I will take pleasure in my weaknesses for your sake, that your power may rest on me. For when I am weak, then I am strong.

Father, thank you that I can do all things through Christ, who strengthens me.

Thank you that you will supply every need of mine according to your riches in glory in Jesus.

Thank you that I can be content in whatever circumstance I am.

You give me the gift of grace according to the working of your power in me.

To you be the glory forever and ever!

JOHN 4:13-14; 6:35; 7:38-39; 1 CORINTHIANS 1:24, 30; 2 CORINTHIANS 12:9-10; EPHESIANS 1:3; 3:7; PHILIPPIANS 4:11, 13, 19-20; 2 PETER 1:3-4

Psalms

Praise the Lord, O my soul!
    All that is within me, praise his holy name!
Praise the Lord, O my soul.
    I don't forget all your benefits, Lord.
You forgive all my sins; you heal all my diseases;
    you redeem my life from destruction.
    You crown me with lovingkindness and tender mercies.
You satisfy my desire with good things,
    so that my youth is renewed like the eagle's.
Lord, you execute righteous acts,
    and justice for all who are oppressed.
You made known your ways to Moses,
    your deeds to the children of Israel.
You are merciful and gracious,
    slow to anger, and abundant in lovingkindness.
You have not dealt with me according to my sins,
    nor repaid me for my iniquities.
For as the heavens are high above the earth,
    so great is your lovingkindness toward those who fear you.
As far as the east is from the west,
    so far have you removed my transgressions from me.
Like a father has compassion on his children,
    so you have compassion on those who fear you.
For you know how I am made; you remember that I am dust.
As for man, his days are like grass;
    the wind passes over it, and it is gone;
    its place remembers it no more.
But your lovingkindness is from everlasting to everlasting
    with those who fear you.
You have established your throne in the heavens.
    Your kingdom rules over all.
Praise the Lord, you his angels, mighty in strength,
    who fulfill his word, obeying the voice of his word.
Praise the Lord, all his armies, you his servants,
    who do his pleasure.
Praise the Lord, all you works of his, in all places of
    his dominion.
Praise the Lord, O my soul!

Psalm 103:1-22

THINGS TO COME

Jesus, to him who overcomes, you will give to eat from the tree of life which is in the Paradise of God.

You will give him the crown of life, and he will not be harmed by the second death.

You will give to him of the hidden manna.

You will give him a white stone, and on the stone a new name written, which no one knows but he who receives it.

You will give him authority over the nations. He will rule them with a rod of iron, shattering them like clay pots, as you also received from your Father.

You will give him the morning star.

You will clothe him in white garments.

You will not blot his name out of the book of life; and you will confess his name before your Father and before his angels.

You will make him a pillar in the temple of God, and he will not go out from there anymore.

You will write on him the name of God, and the name of the city of God, the new Jerusalem, which comes down out of heaven from God, and your new name.

You will give to him to sit down with you on your throne, as you also overcame and sat down with your Father on his throne.

All my thanks to you, Jesus!

REVELATION 2:7, 10-11, 17, 26-28; 3:4-5, 12, 21

22ND SEVEN PRAISES

Shout to the Lord, all you lands!
Come before his presence with singing.
Enter into his gates with thanksgiving,
and into his courts with praise.
Give thanks to him, and bless his name.

PSALM 100:1, 2, 4

THE SOVEREIGN CREATOR OF ALL

Lord, you have not spoken in secret,
    in a land of darkness.
You speak righteousness.
    You declare things that are right.
Those who carry the wood of their engraved image have
        no knowledge;
    they pray to a god that can't save.
Who has shown this from ancient times?
    Who has declared it of old?
    Isn't is you, Lord?
There is no other God besides you, a just God and a Savior.
    There is no one besides you.
You say, "Look to me, and be saved, all the ends of the earth;
    for I am God, and there is no other."
    You have sworn by yourself.
The word has gone out of your mouth in righteousness,
    and will not be revoked,
    that to you every knee shall bow,
    every tongue shall take an oath:
    "There is righteousness and strength only in the I AM."
To you will men come.
    All those who raged against you will be put to shame.
All the offspring of Israel will be justified in you,
    and will rejoice!
Lord, your enemies will fear your name,
    and your glory from the rising of the sun;
For you will come as a rushing stream,
    which your breath drives.
    You are the Redeemer who comes to Zion.

Lord, you have carried me from my birth,
    from the womb.
Even to my old age you are he,
    and even to gray hairs you will carry me.
You have made me, and you will bear me.
    Yes, you will carry me, and will deliver me.

ISAIAH 45:19-25; 46:3-4; 59:19-20

PSALMS

Lord, my God, you are very great.
>You are clothed with honor and majesty.
You cover yourself with light as with a garment.
>You stretch out the heavens like a curtain.
You lay the beams of your rooms in the waters.
>You make the clouds your chariot.
>You walk on the wings of the wind.
You make your messengers winds,
>and your servants flames of fire.
You laid the foundations of the earth,
>that it should not be moved forever.
You covered it with the deep as with a cloak.
>The waters stood above the mountains.
At your rebuke they fled.
>At the voice of your thunder they hurried away.
The mountains rose, the valleys sank down,
>to the place which you had assigned to them.
You have set a boundary that they may not pass over,
>that they don't turn again to cover the earth.
You send springs into the valleys.
>They run among the mountains.
They give drink to every animal of the field.
>The wild donkeys quench their thirst.
The birds of the sky nest by them.
>They sing among the branches.
You water the mountains from your chambers.
>The earth is filled with the fruit of your works.
You cause the grass to grow for the livestock,
>and plants for man to cultivate,
>that he may produce food out of the earth:
Wine that makes the heart of man glad,
>oil to make his face to shine,
>and bread that strengthens man's heart.
Lord, how many are your works!
>In wisdom, you have made them all.

PSALM 104:1-15, 24

THE LOVING AND FAITHFUL GOD

Lord, as the rain comes down and the snow from the sky,
    and doesn't return there, but waters the earth,
    and makes it grow and bud,
    and gives seed to the sower and bread to the eater;
So is your word that goes out of your mouth:
    it will not return to you void,
    but it will accomplish that which you please,
    and it will prosper in the thing you sent it to do.
I will go out with joy,
    and be led out with peace.
The mountains and the hills will break out before us
        into singing;
    and all the trees of the fields will clap their hands.
This will make a name for you, Lord,
    for an everlasting sign that will not be cut off.

Lord, this is the covenant you have made for me. Your Spirit
is on me. You have put your words in my mouth. They will
not depart out of my mouth from now on and forever.

Lord, you are my Savior, my Redeemer, the Mighty One.
    I will greatly rejoice in you!
My soul will be joyful in my God,
    for you have clothed me with the garments of salvation.
You have covered me with the robe of righteousness,
    as a bridegroom decks himself with a garland
    and as a bride adorns herself with her jewels.
For as the earth produces its bud,
    and as the garden causes the things that are sown in it
        to spring up,
    so you, Lord, have caused righteousness and praise to
        spring up.

Lord, I praise you!

ISAIAH 55:10-13; 59:21; 60:16; 61:10-11

FATHER, SON, SPIRIT

Jesus, you are over all, God blessed forever.

The Father promised the good news about you long ago through his prophets in the Holy Scriptures.

You were born of the offspring of David and declared to be the Son of God with power, according to the Spirit of holiness, by the resurrection from the dead.

Through your one righteous act, you brought to all rightness with God, which leads to life.

You are Lord. Through you I have received grace. I have been called to belong to you.

Your good news is the power of God for salvation to everyone who believes. From faith to faith, it reveals the righteousness of God.

You are over all. You are the Lord of all, and you are rich to all who call on you. Whoever calls on your name will be saved.

I confessed with my mouth that you are Lord, and I believed in my heart that God raised you from the dead, and I was saved. As you promised, I will not be disappointed.

You died, rose, and lived again, that you might be Lord of both the dead and the living.

You became a servant to your people for the sake of God's truth, to confirm God's promises to the fathers, and so the Gentiles might glorify God for his mercy.

I give praise to you! I sing to your name. I praise you, Lord. Let all the peoples praise you. You are the root of Jesse, who has arisen to rule over the Gentiles. In you I hope.

Jesus, you accepted me to the glory of God.

Your grace is with me.

ROMANS 1:2-7, 16-17; 5:18; 9:5; 10:9, 12-13; 14:9; 15:7-12; 16:20

CHRIST'S VICTORY

Father, you give life to the dead, and call the things that are not, as though they were. What you promise, you are able to perform. Glory be to you!

Jesus, you are the Son of God. All of God's promises are "Yes" in you.

Father, you are the one who is at work in me. I am your workmanship.

You began a good work in me, and you will bring it to completion until the day of my Lord Jesus Christ.

You called me into fellowship with your Son. You are faithful, and you will confirm me until the end, blameless in the day of Christ.

Father, you are the God of peace. You are able to sanctify me fully, that my whole spirit, soul, and body be preserved complete, blameless at the coming of Jesus. You are the one who called me, and you are faithful. You will bring it to pass.

Thank you that I am a partaker of your grace!

Jesus, I am kept for you.

You are faithful. You will establish me and guard me from the evil one.

You will deliver me from every evil work, and will preserve me for your heavenly Kingdom.

Because of your suffering, I will share in the glory that will be revealed. When you, the chief Shepherd, are revealed, I will receive the crown of glory that doesn't fade away.

Jesus, I love you. I praise you that at your revelation, the proof of my faith will result in praise, glory, and honor.

To you be the glory forever and ever.

ROMANS 4:17, 20, 21; 1 CORINTHIANS 1:6-9; 2 CORINTHIANS 1:18, 20;
EPHESIANS 2:10; PHILIPPIANS 1:6-7; 2:13; 1 THESSALONIANS 5:23-24;
2 TIMOTHY 4:18; 1 PET 1:6; 5:1, 4; JUDE 1:2

PSALMS

Lord, the earth is full of your riches.
You appointed the moon for seasons.
    The sun knows when to set.
You make darkness, and it is night,
    in which all the animals of the forest prowl.
The young lions roar after their prey,
    and seek their food from you.
The sun rises, and they steal away,
    and lie down in their dens.
Man goes out to his work,
    to his labor until the evening.
There is the sea, great and wide,
    in which are living things without number,
    both small and large animals.
There the ships go,
    and leviathan, whom you formed to play there.
These all wait for you,
    that you may give them their food in due season.
You give to them; they gather.
    You open your hand; they are satisfied with good.
You hide your face; they are troubled.
    You take away their breath; they die and return to the dust.
You send out your Spirit and they are created.
    You renew the face of the ground.
Let your glory endure forever.
    May you rejoice in your works.
You look at the earth, and it trembles.
    You touch the mountains, and they smoke.
I will sing to you, Lord, as long as I live.
    I will sing praise to my God while I have my being.
Let my meditation be sweet to you.
    I will rejoice in you.
Bless the Lord, my soul.
    I praise you, Lord!

PSALM 104:19-35

THINGS TO COME

Father, John saw a throne in heaven. You sit on the throne. There is a rainbow around your throne, like an emerald in appearance.

Around your throne are twenty-four thrones, and twenty-four elders sitting, dressed in white garments, with crowns of gold on their heads.

Out from your throne come flashes of lightning, and sounds, and peals of thunder. Seven lamps of fire burn before your throne, which are the seven Spirits of God.

Before the throne is something like a sea of glass, like crystal.

In middle of the throne and around the throne are four living creatures full of eyes in front and behind. The first creature is like a lion, the second like a calf, the third has a face like a man, and the fourth is like a flying eagle.

The four living creatures, each one of them having six wings, are full of eyes around and within. Day and night they do not cease to say,

> "Holy, holy, holy is the Lord God, the Almighty,
> who was and who is and who is to come."

When the living creatures give glory, honor, and thanks to you who sit on the throne, to you who live forever and ever, the twenty-four elders fall down before you who sit on the throne, and worship you who live forever and ever, and throw their crowns before the throne, saying,

> "Worthy are you, our Lord and our God, the Holy One,
> to receive the glory, the honor, and the power;
> for you created all things, and because of your desire
> they existed, and were created."

REVELATION 4:2-11

23rd Seven Praises

Sing to the Lord a new song!
Sing to the Lord, all the earth!
Sing to the Lord!
Bless his name!
Proclaim his salvation from day to day!
Declare his glory among the nations,
his marvelous works among all peoples.
For the Lord is great, and greatly to be praised!
Ascribe to the Lord, you families of nations.
Ascribe to the Lord the glory due his name.

PSALM 96:1-4, 7-8

THE SOVEREIGN CREATOR OF ALL

Who could I compare to you, Lord, and consider your equal,
 as if any could be the same as you?
I think about what you accomplished long ago.
 Truly you are God; you have no peer.
You are God, and there is none like you,
 who announces the end from the beginning
 and reveals beforehand what has not yet occurred,
 who says, "My plan will be realized,
 I will accomplish what I desire."
You summon an eagle from the east,
 from a distant land, one who carries out your plan.
Yes, you have decreed,
 yes, you will bring it to pass;
You have formulated a plan;
 you will carry it out.
You have brought your deliverance near;
 you have brought your salvation near, it does not wait.
You will save and adorn us with splendor.

For your own sake you will act, Lord.
 You will not give your glory to another.
You are he.
 You are the first.
 You are also the last.
Your hand has laid the foundation of the earth,
 and your right hand has spread out the heavens.
 When you call to them, they stand up together.

Heaven is your throne, and the earth is your footstool.
 What kind of house could I build to you?
 Where would you rest?
For your hand has made all these things,
 and so all these things came to be.

I praise you, Lord!

ISAIAH 46:5, 9-13; 48:11-13; 66:1-2

Psalms

I give thanks to you, Lord, for you are good;
    your lovingkindness endures forever.
Let all of your redeemed say so, Lord,
    all of us whom you have redeemed
    from the hand of the adversary.
I cried to you in my trouble,
    and you delivered me out of my distresses,
    and led me by a straight way.
I praise you for your lovingkindness,
    for your wonderful deeds toward me!
You satisfy the longing soul.
    You fill the hungry soul with good.
Lord, some sit in darkness and in the shadow of death,
    because they rebelled against your words,
    and condemned the counsel of the Most High.
They cry to you in their trouble,
    and you save them out of their distresses.
You bring them out of darkness and the shadow of death,
    and break away their chains.
I praise you, Lord, for your lovingkindness,
    for your wonderful deeds to the children of men!
You break the gates of bronze,
    and cut through bars of iron.
Lord, fools are afflicted because of their disobedience,
    and because of their iniquities.
Then they cry to you in their trouble,
    and you save them out of their distresses.
You send your word, and heal them,
    and deliver them from their graves.
I praise you, Lord, for your lovingkindness,
    for your wonderful deeds to the children of men!
I offer you the sacrifice of thanksgiving,
    and declare your deeds with singing.
The earth is full of your lovingkindness, Lord.
    You are good, and do good.

Psalm 107:1-2, 6-22; 119:64, 68

THE LOVING AND FAITHFUL GOD

Jesus, the Lord's Spirit was on you,
    because he anointed you to preach good news to
        the afflicted.
He sent you to bind up the brokenhearted,
    to proclaim liberty to the captives
    and release to those who are bound,
To proclaim the year of his favor
    and the day of vengeance of our God,
    to comfort all who mourn,
    to give to them a garland for ashes,
    the oil of joy instead of mourning,
    the garment of praise for the spirit of heaviness,
That they may be called trees of righteousness,
    the planting of the Lord,
    that he may be glorified.

Lord, you have called me by a new name,
    a name you have given me.
You have made me a crown of beauty in your hand,
    a royal diadem.
I am not called Forsaken anymore,
    but I am called, "My delight is in you,"
For you delight in me,
    and you have betrothed yourself to me.
As a bridegroom rejoices over his bride,
    so you rejoice over me.

I will tell of your lovingkindnesses, Lord, and your praises,
    according to all that you have given me,
And your great goodness toward me,
    which you have given me according to your mercies,
    according to the abundance of your lovingkindness.
I am yours; you are my Savior.
    In all my affliction you have been afflicted.
In your love and mercy you redeemed me.
    You bore me and carried me from long ago.

ISAIAH 61:1-3; 62:2-5; 63:7-9

FATHER, SON, SPIRIT

Holy Spirit, you are the Spirit of Christ.

To the prophets you predicted the sufferings of Christ, and the glories that would follow them.

You have been sent from heaven, and by you the good news is preached. Only by you can someone say, "Jesus is Lord."

You are the Counselor.

In these last days God has poured you out upon all flesh. Sons and daughters prophecy; young men see visions; old men dream dreams.

Holy Spirit, Jesus baptizes in you.

In you we were all baptized into Christ's body. All of its members are one. We were all given to drink of one Spirit—you.

You produce all of the manifestations, distributing to each one separately as you desire. You give various kinds of gifts, but they are all from you.

Your fruit consists in all goodness and righteousness and truth.

You bring unity in the bond of peace.

In your power I am filled with all joy and peace in believing, that I may be full of hope.

Your fellowship, and Jesus's grace, and the Father's love, are with me.

You are the Spirit of glory. I praise you!

MARK 1:10; JOHN 16:9; ACTS 2:17; ROMANS 15:13; 1 CORINTHIANS 3:16; 12:3, 11-13; 2 CORINTHIANS 13:14; EPHESIANS 4:3; 5:9; 1 PETER 1:11-12; 4:12; REVELATION 22:17

CHRIST'S VICTORY

Father, you are able to do exceedingly abundantly above all that I ask or think, according to the power that works in me.

Your surpassingly great power toward me is like the strength you showed when you raised Jesus from the dead, and seated him at your right hand in the heavenlies, far above all rule, authority, power, and dominion.

Father, I declare what great things you have done for me.

Because of you, I am in Christ. You called me. You reconciled me to yourself through Christ. You forgave all my sins.

You washed me, and sanctified me, and justified in me the name of the Lord Jesus, and in your Spirit.

You made me one with yourself and Jesus.

You created my new man, and he is being renewed in your image!

You buried me with Christ. You raised me up with him. You seated me in the heavenlies with Him, so that, in the ages to come, you might show the surpassing riches of your grace toward me.

You called me into your own kingdom and glory. I thank you endlessly!

Now all things are mine, whether the world, or life, or death, or things present, or things to come. All are mine, and I am Christ's, and Christ is yours.

You are the Father of glory. Your inheritance in the saints is overflowing with glory. You have filled me with hope because of my calling in Christ.

I praise you!

LUKE 8:39; JOHN 17:21; 1 CORINTHIANS 1:30; 3:21-23; 6:11, 17;
2 CORINTHIANS 5:18; EPHESIANS 1:17-21; 2:5-7; 3:20; COLOSSIANS 2:11-13;
3:10 11; 1 THESSALONIANS 2:12-13; JUDE 1:1

PSALMS

Lord, I praise you for your lovingkindness,
>for your wonderful deeds for the children of men!

Those who go down to the sea in ships see your deeds,
>and your wonders in the deep.

For you command, and raise the stormy wind,
>which lifts up its waves.

They mount up to the sky; they go down again to the depths.
>Their soul melts away because of trouble.

Then they cry to you in their trouble,
>and you bring them out of their distress.

You make the storm a calm and still the waves.
>You bring them to their desired haven.

Let them exalt you in the assembly of the people,
>and praise you in the seat of the elders!

Lord, you turn rivers into a desert,
>springs of water into a thirsty ground,
>and a fruitful land into a salt waste,
>for the wickedness of those who dwell in it.

You turn a desert into a pool of water,
>and a dry land into water springs.

There you make the hungry live,
>that they may prepare a city to live in, sow fields,
>plant vineyards, and reap the fruits of increase.

You bless them, so that they are multiplied greatly.

You pour contempt on princes,
>and cause them to wander in a trackless waste.

Yet you lift the needy out of their affliction,
>and increase their families like a flock.

The upright will see it, and be glad.
>All the wicked will shut their mouths.

Whoever is wise will give heed,
>and consider your lovingkindness, Lord!

I praise you!

PSALM 107:23-43

THINGS TO COME

Jesus, you are the Lion from the tribe of Judah, the Root of David. You have overcome. You open the book and its seven seals.

John saw you in the middle of the throne, and of the four living creatures. You were a Lamb standing, as though you had been slain, having seven horns and seven eyes, which are the seven Spirits of God, sent out into all the earth.

You took the book out of the right hand of him who sits on the throne, and the four living creatures and the twenty-four elders fell down before you, each one having a harp, and golden bowls full of incense, which are the prayers of the saints. They sang a new song, saying,

> "You are worthy to take the book
>   and to open its seals:
> For you were killed,
>   and bought for God with your blood
>   people out of every tribe, language, people,
>   and nation.
> You have made them to be kings and priests to you,
>   and they will reign on the earth."

John heard the voice of many angels around the throne, the living creatures, and the elders. The number of them was ten thousands of ten thousands. They said with a loud voice,

> "Worthy is the Lamb who was slain to receive power,
> wealth, wisdom, might, honor, glory, and blessing!"

And every created thing which is in heaven and on the earth and under the earth and on the sea, and all things in them, said,

> "To him who sits on the throne, and to the Lamb,
> be blessing, honor, glory, and dominion forever and ever."

The four living creatures said, "Amen." And the elders fell down and worshiped you, Jesus.

REVELATION 5:5-14

24TH SEVEN PRAISES

*Stand up and bless the Lord your God
from everlasting to everlasting!
Blessed be your glorious name,
which is exalted above all blessing and praise!*

NEHEMIAH 9:5

THE SOVEREIGN CREATOR OF ALL

Lord, you are the one who comes in glorious apparel,
    marching in the greatness of your strength.
It is you, you who speak in righteousness,
    mighty to save.

I stand before you in awe.
You placed the sand to be a boundary for the sea,
    a permanent barrier that it can never cross.
Its waves may toss, but they can never prevail.
    Though they roar, they still can't pass over it.

There is no one like you, LORD.
    You are great, and your name is great in might.
Who shouldn't fear you, King of all nations?
    Reverence belongs to you.
Among all the wise men of the nations, and all their kings,
    there is no one like you.

Lord, you are the only true God.
    You are the living God and an everlasting King.
At your wrath, the earth trembles.
    The nations can't withstand your indignation.

The gods of the nations didn't make heaven and earth.
    They will perish from the earth and from under
        the heavens.
You are the one who by your power made the earth.
    You are the one who by your wisdom established
        the world,
    and by your understanding stretched out the heavens.
When you utter your voice, the waters in the heavens roar.
    You cause the vapors to ascend from the ends of
        the earth.
You make lightning flash in the rain.
    You bring the wind out of your storehouses.
You are the Maker of all things.
    Lord of the Armies is your name.

ISAIAH 63:1; JEREMIAH 5:22; 10:6-7, 10-13, 16

PSALMS

My heart is steadfast, God.
>   I will sing and I will make music with my soul.
Wake up, harp and lyre!
>   I will wake up the dawn.
I will give thanks to you, God, among the nations.
>   I will sing praises to you among the peoples.
For your lovingkindness is great above the heavens.
>   Your faithfulness reaches to the skies.
Be exalted, God, above the heavens!
>   Let your glory be over all the earth.
Through you I will do valiantly.
>   For you will tread down my enemies.

Lord, you are the God of my praise.
>   Your lovingkindness is good.
With my lips I will praise you abundantly;
>   I will praise you among the multitude.
For you stand at the right hand of the needy,
>   to save him from those who condemn him.

Jesus, the Father said to you,
>   "Sit at my right hand,
>   until I make your enemies a footstool for your feet."
God will send the rod of your strength out of Zion.
>   You will rule among your enemies.
The Father has sworn, and will not change his mind:
>   "You are a priest forever in the order of Melchizedek."
The Lord is at your right hand.
>   He will crush kings in the day of his wrath.
He will judge among the nations.
>   He will crush the rulers of the whole earth.

I praise you, Lord!

PSALM 108:1-5, 13; 109:1, 21, 30-31; 110:1-2, 4-6

THE LOVING AND FAITHFUL GOD

You, Lord, are my Father.
> My Redeemer from everlasting is your name.
Since days of old men have not heard, nor perceived by
> the ear,
>> nor has the eye seen a God besides you,
>> who acts on behalf of those who wait for you.

You allowed me to seek you, though I didn't ask for you.
> You allowed me to find you, though I didn't seek you.
> You said, "Here I am," when I didn't even call on
>> your name.
Before you formed me in my mother's womb you chose me.
> Before I was born you set me apart.

I come to you. You are my God. My salvation is in you.
Lord, if people want to glory, they should glory in this:
> that they understand and know you,
That you are the I AM, who exercises lovingkindness, justice,
> and righteousness in the earth.
> These are the things you delight in.

Lord, you are with me as a dread champion.
> Therefore my persecutors will stumble and won't prevail.
They will be utterly disappointed,
> even with an everlasting dishonor which will never
>> be forgotten.
You, my Redeemer, are strong:
> The God of Armies is your name.
> You champion my cause.

Your lovingkindness never ceases;
> your compassion never comes to an end.
They are new every morning.
> Great is your faithfulness.
You are my portion, Lord; therefore I hope in you.
> You are good to those who wait for you,
> to the soul who seeks you.

You have loved me with an everlasting love.
> You have drawn me with lovingkindness.

LAMENTATIONS 3:22-25; ISAIAH 63:16; 64:4; 65:1; JEREMIAH 1:5; 3:22-23; 9:24;
20:11; 31:3; 50:34

FATHER, SON, SPIRIT

Father, every good thing and every perfect gift is from you. You are the Father of lights. With you there is no variation. You give to all liberally and without reproach.

You can't be tempted by evil, and you yourself tempt no one.

You chose those who are poor in this world to be rich in faith, and heirs of the kingdom which you promised to those who love you.

You are my God and Father; you made me in your image.

You are the only Lawgiver and Judge, who is able to save and to destroy. You are full of compassion and mercy.

You are the Father of my Lord Jesus Christ. I am foreknown by you.

Father, you are holy. You are gracious. You are a faithful Creator.

Your word, the good news preached to me, endures forever.

In all things, may you be glorified through Jesus Christ. To him belong the glory and the dominion forever and ever!

You give grace to the humble. Your hand is mighty. You will exalt me in due time. I cast my worries on you, because you care for me.

You are the God of all grace. You called me to your eternal glory in Christ Jesus. To you be the glory and the power forever and ever.

Father, you are from the beginning. You are light, and in you is no darkness at all. You know all things.

You sent the Son to be the Savior of the world.

From you, Father, and from Jesus, your Son, grace, mercy, and truth are with me. Through you the truth remains with me, and will be with me forever.

JAMES 1:5, 13, 17; 2:5; 3:9; 4:6, 12; 5:11; 1 PETER 1:2-3, 16, 22, 24; 4:11, 19; 5:5-7, 10; 1 JOHN 1:2-3, 5; 2:13; 3:20; 4:14

CHRIST'S VICTORY

Father, thank you that I, who am in Christ, am a new creation!

That which is born of the flesh is flesh. That which is born of the Spirit is spirit. I am born of you!

The old things have passed away. All things have become new. Now all things are from you!

Father, you have given me a new heart, and put a new spirit within me. You have taken away the stony heart out of my flesh, and have given me a heart of flesh.

In Christ, you have made me complete.

You created my new self. My new self has been created in true righteousness and holiness.

You made Jesus, who knew no sin, to be sin on my behalf, that I might become the righteousness of God in him!

Jesus, through one man's disobedience I was made a sinner; through your obedience I have been made righteous.

I am born of you, Father. I, who practice righteousness, am righteous, just as Jesus is righteous.

You have made me a partaker of the divine nature.
You have made me a child of Light.
You have sanctified me and made me holy.
You have made me blameless.
You have made me a saint.
You have made me alive to you.
You have made me one spirit with you.
You have made me a fragrance of Christ to you.

You have perfected me for all time.

Father, I praise you!

EZEKIEL 36:26; JOHN 1:13; 3:6; ROMANS 5:19; 6:11; 1 CORINTHIANS 1:2; 6:17; 2 CORINTHIANS 2:15; 5:17-18, 21; EPHESIANS 4:24; COLOSSIANS 1:22; 2:10; 3:10, 12; 1 THESSALONIANS 5:5; HEBREWS 10:14; 1 PETER 1:4; 1 JOHN 2:29; 3:7, 9

PSALMS

I praise you, Lord!
>I give thanks to you with my whole heart,
>in the council of the upright, and in the congregation.

Your works are great,
>pondered by all those who delight in them.

Your work is splendor and majesty.
>Your righteousness endures forever.

You have caused your wonderful works to be remembered.
>You are gracious and merciful.

You give food to those who revere you.
>You always remember your covenant.

You have shown your people the power of your works,
>in giving them the heritage of the nations.

The works of your hands are truth and justice.
>All your precepts are sure.

They are established forever and ever.
>They are done in truth and uprightness.

You have sent redemption to your people.
>You have ordained your covenant forever.
>Your name is holy and awesome!

The fear of you, Lord, is the beginning of wisdom.
>Your praise endures forever!

Those who trust in you, Lord, are as Mount Zion,
>which can't be moved, but remains forever.

As the mountains surround Jerusalem,
>so you surround your people from this time forward
>>and forevermore.

Lord, your word is settled in heaven forever.
>Your faithfulness is to all generations.

You have established the earth, and it remains.
>All things serve you.

PSALM 111:1-10; 119:89-91; 125:1-2

THINGS TO COME

Father, with a loud voice those around the throne will cry out,

> "Salvation to our God who sits on the throne,
> and to the Lamb."

All the angels and the elders and the four living creatures
will fall on their faces before the throne and worship
God, saying,

> "Amen! Blessing, glory, wisdom, thanksgiving,
> honor, power and might, be to our God forever
> and ever. Amen."

Jesus, because of you, I am made white in the blood of
the Lamb.

I will hunger no longer, nor thirst anymore; nor will the
sun beat down on me, nor any heat; for you, the Lamb in
the center of the throne, will be my shepherd. You will guide
me to springs of life-giving waters. And God, you will wipe
every tear from my eyes.

Lord, John saw a mighty angel coming down out of the sky,
clothed with a cloud. His face was like the sun, and his feet
like pillars of fire. He set his right foot on the sea, and his
left on the land.

He cried with a loud voice and swore by you, who live
forever and ever, who created heaven and the things that are
in it, the earth and the things that are in it, and the sea and
the things that are in it, that there would no longer be delay,
but that when the voice of the seventh angel sounded, then
the mystery of God, as you declared to your prophets, would
be finished.

I praise you, Lord!

REVELATION 7:10-12, 14-17; 10:1-7

25TH SEVEN PRAISES

I will praise you, Lord my God, with my whole heart.
I will glorify your name forevermore.

PSALM 86:12

The Sovereign Creator of All

Lord, you are the transcendent God, near at hand and far off.
Can anyone hide in secret places so that you can't see him?
For you fill heaven and earth.

You are the God of hosts. You made the earth, and people,
and the animals on the earth by your great power and
outstretched arm. You give it to whomever you wish.

You are the one who gives the sun for a light by day,
    and the ordinances of the moon and of the stars for a
       light by night,
Who stirs up the sea, so that its waves roar;
    Lord of the Armies is your name.

You have made the earth by your power.
    You have established the world by your wisdom.
    By your understanding you have stretched out the
       heavens.
When you utter your voice,
    there is a roar of waters in the heavens,
    and you cause the vapors to ascend from the ends of
       the earth.
You make lightning for the rain,
    and bring the wind out of your treasuries.

Shall any teach you knowledge, God,
    since you judge those who are high?
You are exalted in your power.
    Who is a teacher like you?
    Who has prescribed your way for you?
You are great;
    the number of your years is unsearchable.

Lord, you are the one who created all things;
    Lord of the Armies is your name.

You, O Lord, reign forever.
    Your throne is from generation to generation.

Job 21:22; 36:22-23, 26; Jeremiah 23:23-24; 27:4-5; 31:35; 51:15-16, 19;
Lamentations 5:19

PSALMS

I praise you, Lord!
  I praise your name.
Blessed be your name
  from this time forward and forevermore.
From the rising of the sun to its going down,
  your name is to be praised.
Lord, you are high above all nations;
  your glory is above the heavens.
Who is like you, O Lord my God?
  Your seat is on high.
  You stoop down to see in heaven and in the earth.
You raise up the poor out of the dust.
  You lift up the needy from the ash heap,
That you may set him with princes,
  even with the princes of his people.
You settle the barren woman in her home
  as a joyful mother of children.
I praise you, Lord!

Praise the Lord, all you nations!
  Extol him, all you peoples!
For your lovingkindness is great toward us, Lord.
  Your faithfulness endures forever.
I praise you, Lord!

Blessed be you, Lord.
  My help is in your name,
  you who made heaven and earth.

Lord, you are faithful and righteous and full of
    lovingkindness.
  Your Spirit is good.

I praise you!

PSALM 113:1-9; 117:1-2; 124:6, 8; 143:1, 8, 10

THE LOVING AND FAITHFUL GOD

Lord God, the great I AM: you have made the heavens and the earth by your great power and by your outstretched arm. There is nothing too hard for you.

The great, the mighty God, Lord of Hosts is your name: great in counsel, and mighty in work; your eyes are open to all the ways of men.

You show unfailing love.

You performed signs and wonders in the land of Egypt and made yourself a name. You brought your people Israel out of the land of Egypt with signs, with wonders, with a strong hand, with an outstretched arm, and with great terror. You gave them the land that you swore to their fathers, a land flowing with milk and honey.

Lord, you made a new covenant with the house of Israel and Judah, not like the covenant you made when you took them out of Egypt. This is the new covenant you made:

> You put your law into our inward parts,
>   and write it on our hearts.
> You are our God,
>   and we are your people.
> We will no longer each teach our neighbor,
>   and every man teach his brother, saying,
>   "Know the Lord";
> For all of us know you,
>   from our least to our greatest.
> For you have forgiven our iniquity,
>   and you remember our sin no more.

You have put a new spirit within me. You have taken the stony heart out of my flesh, and given me a heart of flesh, that I might walk in your ways. I am yours, and you are my God.

I praise you!

JEREMIAH 31:31-34; 32:17-22; EZEKIEL 11:19-20

FATHER, SON, SPIRIT

Jesus, you have been made to me wisdom from God, and righteousness, and sanctification, and redemption. I boast in you.

In everything I have been enriched in you, as I wait for your revelation.

You are the power of God and the wisdom of God.

I don't know anything except you and you crucified. My faith doesn't stand in the wisdom of men, but in the power of God.

You are the only foundation which could be laid. You are the spiritual rock that all the Hebrews drank from in the wilderness. You are my Passover, who has been sacrificed in my place.

Jesus, there is one God, the Father, of whom are all things, and I am for him; and one Lord, Jesus Christ, through whom are all things, and I live through you.

You are one body, with many members. We are your members.

In one Spirit we were baptized into you.

We are your body, and individually members of you. My own body is a member of you. May you be glorified in my body and my spirit, which are yours.

Jesus, the first man, Adam, became a living soul. You, the last Adam, became a life-giving spirit.

The first man was of the earth, made of dust. You, the second man, are the Lord from heaven. As I have borne the image of the one made of dust, so I will bear the image of you, the man of heaven.

Jesus, you are the Son of God. In you is the "Yes" to all the promises of God. Through you is my "Amen" to the glory of God through me.

I praise you!

1 CORINTHIANS 1:3-5, 24-25; 30-31; 2:2, 5; 3:11; 5:7; 6:15, 20; 8:6; 10:4; 12:12-13, 28; 15:45-49; 2 CORINTHIANS 1:18, 20

CHRIST'S VICTORY

Father, I was dead in sins.

I once walked according to the course of this world, according to the prince of the power of the air, the spirit who now works in the children of disobedience. I lived in the lusts of my flesh, doing the desires of the flesh and of the mind.

I was by nature a child of wrath.

But you are rich in mercy. Because of your great love with which you loved me, even when I was dead in my sins, you made me alive together with Christ. You saved me by your grace!

You raised me up with him, and seated me with him in the heavenlies in Christ Jesus, so in the ages to come you might show how exceedingly rich your grace is and your kindness is toward me in Christ.

Father, I praise you!

Jesus, I was separate from you. I was a stranger to the covenant of promise. I had no hope and was without God in the world.

I lived in the futility of my mind, darkened in my understanding, alienated from the life of God because of the ignorance that was in me, because of my hard heart.

But now, in you, through your blood, I who was once far off have been brought near. Through you I have bold and confident access through the Spirit to the Father.

Because of you, I am no longer a stranger and an alien. I am a fellow citizen with all the saints. I am part of God's household.

I have put on the new man, created in the likeness of God, truly righteous and holy. I was once darkness, but now I am light in the Lord.

Jesus, I praise you!

EPHESIANS 2:1-7, 12-14, 18-19; 3:12; 4:17-18, 4:24; 5:8

PSALMS

The earth trembles at your presence, Lord,
>   at the presence of God.
Lord, where does my help come from?
>   It comes from you,
>   who made heaven and earth.
You will not allow my foot to be moved.
>   You who keep me will not slumber.
Lord, you are my keeper,
>   my shade on my right hand.
The sun will not harm me by day,
>   nor the moon by night.
You, Lord, will keep me from all evil.
>   You will keep my soul.
You will guard my going out and my coming in,
>   from this time forward, and forevermore.

This is the day that you have made.
>   I will rejoice and be glad in it!
You are the Lord, God.
>   You have given me light.
You are my God, and I give thanks to you.
>   You are my God; I exalt you.
I give thanks to you, Lord, for you are good;
>   your lovingkindness endures forever.

Lord, you are my God;
>   you are the strength of my salvation.
You maintain the cause of the afflicted,
>   and justice for the needy.
Surely the righteous will give thanks to your name;
>   the upright will dwell in your presence.

PSALM 114:7; 118:24-29; 121:1-8; 140:6-7, 12-13

THINGS TO COME

Father, great voices in heaven said,

> "The kingdom of the world has become the kingdom
> of our Lord, and of his Christ. He will reign forever
> and ever!"

The twenty-four elders, who sit on their thrones before you,
fell on their faces and worshiped you, saying:

> "We give you thanks, Lord God, the Almighty, the one
> who is and who was; because you have taken your
> great power and have begun to reign. The nations were
> enraged, and your wrath came. So did the time for the
> dead to be judged, and to give your bondservants, the
> prophets, their reward, as well as to the saints, and those
> who fear your name, to the small and the great, and to
> destroy those who destroy the earth."

Your temple in heaven was opened, and the ark of your
covenant was seen in your temple. Lightnings, sounds,
thunders, an earthquake, and great hail followed.

Jesus, there was a loud voice in heaven, saying,

> "Now the salvation, the power, and the kingdom of
> our God, and the authority of his Christ have come;
> for the accuser of our brothers has been thrown down,
> who accuses them before our God day and night. They
> overcame him because of the Lamb's blood, and because
> of the word of their testimony. They didn't love their life,
> even to death. Therefore rejoice, heavens, and you who
> dwell in them."

Jesus, I praise you!

Thank you that my name has been written from the foundation
of the world in the book of life of the Lamb who was slain.

REVELATION 11:15-19; 12:10-12; 13:8

26TH SEVEN PRAISES

Oh come, let's sing to the Lord.
Let's shout aloud to the rock of our salvation!
Let's come into his presence with thanksgiving.
Let's extol him with songs!
Oh come, let's worship and bow down.
Let's kneel before the Lord, our Maker!

PSALM 95:1, 2, 6

The Sovereign Creator of All

Lord, the heavens were opened to Ezekiel, and he saw visions of you.

He saw a stormy wind and a great cloud, with flashing lightning, and a brightness around it, and fire with glowing metal at its center.

Four living creatures were there with the likeness of men. Each had four wings, and four faces: that of a man, and a lion, and an ox, and an eagle.

Their appearance was like burning coals of fire, like torches. Fire went up and down among them and lightning went out of the fire. The living creatures moved like flashes of lightning.

There were four wheels on the earth beside the living creatures. They appeared as a wheel within a wheel. Their rims were high and dreadful, full of eyes all around.

When the living creatures moved, the wheels went beside them. When they were lifted up from the earth, the wheels were lifted up, for the spirit of the living creatures was in the wheels.

When the creatures moved, Ezekiel heard the noise of their wings like the noise of great waters, like the voice of you, the Almighty, a roar like the sound of an army.

Stretched out over the heads of the living creatures there was the likeness of an expanse, like an awesome crystal. There was a voice above the expanse, and the likeness of a throne, like a sapphire stone.

On it was the likeness of the appearance of a man. From your waist up, there was glowing metal; and from your waist down there was appearance of fire. Brightness was all around you, like that of a rainbow.

This was the appearance of the likeness of the glory of you, Lord, the I AM.

I praise you!

Ezekiel 1:1-28

Psalms

Not to us, Lord, not to us,
    but to your name give glory,
    for your lovingkindness, and for your truth's sake.
Why should the nations say,
    "Where is their God?"
My God is in the heavens.
    Lord, you do whatever you please.
The nations' idols are silver and gold,
    the work of men's hands.
They have mouths, but they don't speak.
    They have eyes, but they don't see.
They have ears, but they don't hear.
    They have noses, but they don't smell.
They have hands, but they don't feel.
    They have feet, but they don't walk,
    neither do they speak through their throat.
Those who make them will be like them;
    yes, everyone who trusts in them.
Lord, I will trust in you!
    You are my help and my shield.
You will bless those who fear you,
    both small and great.
I am blessed by you, Lord,
    who made heaven and earth.
The heavens are your heavens, Lord,
    but you have given the earth to the children of men.
I will bless you
    from this time forward and forevermore.
I praise you, Lord!

Psalm 115:1-18

THE LOVING AND FAITHFUL GOD

Lord, you have entered into a marriage covenant with us, and we became yours. You have established an everlasting covenant with us. You are the Lord God. You yourself have made atonement for us.

You have given me a new heart, and put a new spirit within me. You have taken away the stony heart out of my flesh, and have given me a heart of flesh. You have put your Spirit within me, and you cause me to walk in your ways.

Lord, you cleanse me from all my iniquities. You put your Spirit in me, and I live. You are the one who does it. I know that you are God. You do not hide your face from me. You have poured out your Spirit on me, as you declared.

You are my God. You are with me. I am yours. I am the sheep of your pasture. I am in your covenant, a covenant of peace.

Lord, you save your flock. You set up one Shepherd over us, your Prince who feeds us. He is my Shepherd.

You yourself are the Shepherd of your sheep, and you cause us to lie down. You seek that which was lost, and bring back that which was driven away. You bind up that which was broken, and strengthen those who were sick.

Lord, you will magnify your great name. The nations will know that you are the Lord God, when you magnify yourself in us before their eyes. You have sprinkled clean water on us, and made us clean.

I praise you!

Ezekiel 16:8, 60, 63; 34:15-16, 22-23, 25, 30-31; 36:24-27, 33; 37:14; 39:28-29

FATHER, SON, SPIRIT

My soul magnifies you, Lord.
    My spirit rejoices in you, God, my Savior,
    for you are mighty and have done great things for me.
Holy is your name.
    Your mercy is for generations and generations on those
        who fear you.
You have shown strength with your arm.
    You have scattered the proud in the imagination of
        their hearts.
You have put down princes from their thrones,
    and have exalted the lowly.
You have filled the hungry with good things.
    You have sent the rich away empty.
You have given us help.
    You have remembered mercy
        to Abraham and his offspring forever.
Blessed be you, Lord,
    for have redeemed your people;
You raised up a horn of salvation for us
        in the house of your servant David,
    salvation from our enemies and from the hand of all
        who hate us;
To show mercy to us,
    to remember your holy covenant,
The oath which you swore to Abraham,
    to grant to us that we,
    being delivered out of the hand of our enemies,
    should serve you without fear,
    in holiness and righteousness before you all the days of
        our life.
You are the Most High;
    you provide salvation to your people by the forgiveness
        of our sins,
Because of your tender mercy
        by which the sunrise from on high visits us,
    to shine on those who sit in darkness and the shadow
        of death;
    to guide our feet into the way of peace.

LUKE 1:46-55, 68-79

CHRIST'S VICTORY

Father, I was once foolish, disobedient, deceived, enslaved to various lusts and pleasures, living in malice and envy. Others hated me and I hated them.

But my God and Savior, when your kindness and your love toward me appeared, you saved me.

It wasn't by my works of righteousness, but by your mercy, through the washing of regeneration and renewing by the Holy Spirit. You poured him out on me richly through Jesus Christ my Savior.

I was made right with you, so I might be an heir according to the hope of eternal life.

I give you thanks, because you delivered me out of the domain of darkness, and transferred me into the kingdom of your beloved Son. In him I have redemption, the forgiveness of my sins.

You have qualified me to be a partaker of the inheritance of the saints in light.

Father, I praise you!

Jesus, in my evil deeds I was alienated from you. I was your enemy in my mind. But you reconciled me in your fleshly body through death. You did this to present me holy and without defect and blameless before you.

I was dead in my sins, but you made me alive together with you.

You forgave me all my sins. You cancelled out the record of debt I had to you, nailing it to the cross.

You circumcised me with a circumcision made without hands. You buried me with you, and you raised me with you.

I no longer belong to the darkness. You have made me a child of light!

Jesus, I praise you!

COLOSSIANS 1:12-14, 21-22; 2:11-14; 1 THESSALONIANS 5:4-5; TITUS 3:3-7

PSALMS

I love you, Lord, because you listen to my voice,
   and my cries for mercy.
Because you have turned your ear to me,
   I will call on you as long as I live.
   The cords of death surrounded me;
   I found trouble and sorrow.
Then I called on your name:
   "Lord, deliver my soul."
Lord, you are gracious and righteous.
   Yes, my God is merciful.
You preserve the simple.
   I was brought low, and you saved me.
Return to your rest, my soul,
   for God has dealt bountifully with you.
For you have delivered my soul from death, Lord,
   my eyes from tears,
   and my feet from falling.
What will I give to you for all your benefits toward me?
   I will take the cup of salvation, and call on your name.
I will offer to you the sacrifice of thanksgiving,
   and will call on your name.
I praise you, Lord!

Lord, there is forgiveness with you, and lovingkindness,
      and redemption.
   You have redeemed me from all my sins.
You have done great things for me,
   and I am glad.
I have sown in tears, but I will reap in joy.

Ps 116:1-8, 12-13, 17, 19; 126:3-4; 130:4, 7, 8

THINGS TO COME

A great multitude in heaven will praise you, Father, saying,

> "Hallelujah! Salvation, power, and glory belong to our
> God, because his judgments are true and righteous."

You will judge the great prostitute, the great city, Babylon,
who corrupts the earth with her sexual immorality, and you
will avenge the blood of your servants at her hand.

You who will judge her are strong. In one day her judgment
will come: plagues and pestilence and mourning and
famine, and she will be burned up with fire.

The heavens will rejoice, with all the saints, apostles, and
prophets, for you, God, will pronounce judgment for us on
her. Hallelujah! For the smoke will rise up from her forever
and ever.

Father, the twenty-four elders and the four living creatures
will fall down and worship you who sit on the throne,
saying,

> "Hallelujah! Give praise to our God, all you his servants,
> you who fear him, the small and the great!"

Jesus, there will be a voice of a great multitude, like the roar
of many waters, like the sound of mighty thunders, saying,

> "Hallelujah! For the Lord our God, the Almighty, reigns!
> Let's rejoice and be exceedingly glad, and let's give the
> glory to him. For the wedding of the Lamb has come,
> and his bride has made herself ready."

Jesus, how blessed we are who are invited to the wedding
supper of the Lamb!

REVELATION 18:8, 20; 19:1-9

27TH SEVEN PRAISES

I will praise the name of God with a song,
and will magnify him with thanksgiving.
Let heaven and earth praise him;
the seas, and everything that moves in them!

PSALM 69:30, 34

THE SOVEREIGN CREATOR OF ALL

Lord, your glory comes. Your voice is like the sound of many
waters, and the earth is illuminated with your glory.

May your name be blessed forever and ever;
    wisdom and might are yours.
You change the times and the seasons.
    You remove kings and set up kings.
You give wisdom to the wise,
    and knowledge to those who have understanding.
You reveal the deep and secret things.
    You know what is in the darkness,
    and the light dwells with you.
I thank you and praise you, O God.
    You have given me wisdom and might.

Lord, you are the God of heaven. You have set up an
everlasting kingdom which will never be destroyed, nor will
its sovereignty be left to another. It breaks in pieces and
consumes all kingdoms, but it will stand forever.

You are the great God. You are the God of gods and the Lord
of kings, the revealer of mysteries.

Lord, you are the Most High God.
How great are your signs!
    How mighty are your wonders!
Your kingdom is an everlasting kingdom,
    your dominion from generation to generation.

You, Most High, rule in the kingdoms of men, and you give
them to whomever you will.

Your glory fills your temple. Blessed be your glory! Your
court is filled with its brightness.

I praise you!

EZEKIEL 3:12; 10:5; 43:2, 5; DANIEL 2:20-23, 44-45, 47; 4:2-3, 17

PSALMS

I give thanks to you, Lord, for you are good;
>   your lovingkindness endures forever.
You are on my side.
>   I will not be afraid.
>   What can man do to me?
You are on my side,
>   therefore I will look in triumph at my enemies.
It is better to take refuge in you, Lord,
>   than to put confidence in man.
It is better to take refuge in you,
>   than to put confidence in princes.
You, Lord, are my strength and song.
>   You have become my salvation.
The voice of rejoicing and salvation is with the righteous.
>   Your right hand, Lord, does valiantly.
Your right hand is exalted!
>   I will live and declare your works.
I will enter into the gates of righteousness
>   and give thanks to you.
This is your gate, Lord.
>   The righteous enter into it.
I give thanks to you, for you have answered me,
>   and have become my salvation.
The stone which the builders rejected
>   has become the cornerstone.
This is your doing, Lord.
>   It is marvelous in my eyes.

Great are your tender mercies, Lord.
>   Seven times a day I praise you.

PSALM 118:1-23; 119:156, 164

THE LOVING AND FAITHFUL GOD

I praise and extol and honor you, King of heaven. All your works are truth, and your ways justice.

O, Lord, the great and awesome God, you keep covenant and lovingkindness with those who love you. Righteousness belongs to you, Lord, and mercy and forgiveness.

You are God, and not man, the Holy One.

You do not come to me in wrath.

You have allured me.
    You have brought me into the wilderness,
    and spoken tenderly to me.
I am not a slave anymore; you have wed me to you.
    You have betrothed me to you forever.
    You have betrothed me to you in righteousness, in justice,
    in lovingkindness, and in compassion.
You have betrothed me to you in faithfulness,
    so I can know you.
You have had mercy on me who had not obtained mercy;
    you have called me yours, who was not yours,
    so I can say, you are my God.

Lord, you come and rain righteousness on me.

When I was a child, you loved me.
    You taught me to walk.
You took me by my arms;
    you healed me.
You drew me with ties of love;
    you lifted the yoke from me;
    you bent down to feed me.
You said, "How can I give you up?
    My heart is turned over within me,
    My tender compassion is aroused."

I praise you!

DANIEL 4:37; 9:4, 7, 9; HOSEA 2:14-16, 19-20, 23; 10:12; 11:1-4, 8-9

Father, Son, Spirit

Jesus, the Father created all things through you.

You are seated in the heavenlies, far above all rule, authority, power, dominion, and every name that is named, not only in this age, but also in the one to come.

The Father put all things in subjection under your feet, and gave you to be head over all things for the Church.

The Church is your body, the fullness of you who fills all in all.

You are the chief cornerstone of God's whole household. The whole building is being fitted together and is growing into a holy temple of God—the place where God himself dwells in the Spirit.

You are the Savior of the body.

You have made me a fellow heir, a fellow member of your body, a fellow partaker of the promise in you through the good news.

Jesus, in you are unsearchable riches.

You are full of tender compassion toward me.

The fruit of righteousness comes through you, to the glory and praise of God.

Thank you that you have granted me, not only to believe in you, but also to suffer for you.

Jesus, I rejoice in you! I have no confidence in the flesh, but I rejoice in you!

Whatever things were gain to me, I count them as loss now. Everything is a loss compared to the excellency of knowing you.

Jesus, I rejoice in you always! Thank you that your grace is with me.

I love you with an incorruptible love.

Ephesians 1:20-23; 2:20-22; 3:6, 9; 5:23; 6:24; Philippians 1:8, 11, 29; 3:1, 3, 7, 8; 4:1, 23

CHRIST'S VICTORY

Jesus, you are my great high priest who has passed through the heavens, the Son of God.

You were faithful to the One who appointed you. You didn't glorify yourself by making yourself a high priest. Rather, the Father declared,

> "You are my Son.
> You are a priest forever."

You became my high priest, not because of your physical ancestry, but because of the power of your indestructible life.

Father, thank you that you set aside the former commandment, the law, because it was weak and useless and made nothing perfect. Instead, you brought me a better hope, my great high priest. Through him I draw near to you.

Jesus, you became flesh and blood like me, so through death you might bring to nothing the one who had the power of death, the devil. You delivered all of us, because through our fear of death we were all our lifetime in bondage.

You sympathize with my weaknesses, because you were tempted in all points just like I am, yet without sin.

Because you yourself suffered temptation, you are able to help me when I am tempted.

Jesus, through you I draw near with boldness to the throne of grace, and you provide mercy and grace to help me in time of need.

You are my merciful and faithful high priest, because in all things you were made like me.

I praise you, Jesus!

HEBREWS 2:14-15, 17-18; 4:15-16; 5:5-6; 7:15-16, 18-19

PSALMS

I praise you, Lord!
>I praise your name!

I praise you, Lord, for you are good.
>I sing praises to your name, for that is pleasant.
>You have chosen me to be your own.

I know that you are great,
>that you, Lord, are above all gods.

Whatever you please, you do,
>in heaven and in earth, in the seas and in all deeps.

You cause the clouds to rise from the ends of the earth.
>You make lightning come with the rain.
>You bring the wind out of your storehouses.

Your name, Lord, endures forever;
>your fame throughout all generations.

The idols of the nations are silver and gold,
>the work of men's hands.

They have mouths, but they can't speak.
>They have eyes, but they can't see.

They have ears, but they can't hear,
>neither is there any breath in their mouths.

Those who make them will be like them,
>yes, everyone who trusts in them.

But I praise you, Lord!
>May everyone who fears you give you praise.

Blessed be you, Lord.
>I praise you!

Lord, you are my refuge,
>my portion in the land of the living.

You will be good to me.

PSALM 135:1-7, 13-21; 142:5, 7

THINGS TO COME

Jesus, heaven will be opened, and there will be a white horse. You who sit on it are called Faithful and True.

In righteousness you judge and make war. Your eyes are a flame of fire, and on your head are many crowns.

You have a name written which no one knows but you yourself. You are clothed in a garment dipped in blood. Your name is called The Word of God.

The armies which are in heaven follow you on white horses. They are clothed in white, pure, fine linen.

Out of your mouth proceeds a sharp, double-edged sword, that with it you may strike down the nations. You will rule them a rod of iron. You tread the wine press of the fierce wrath of God, the Almighty.

On your garment and on your thigh you have a name written,

    "KING OF KINGS, AND LORD OF LORDS."

The beast and the kings of the earth, and their armies, will gather together to make war against you, and against your army.

The beast and the false prophet will be thrown alive into the lake of fire that burns with sulfur. The rest will be killed with your sword, the sword which comes out of your mouth.

King of Kings, I praise you!

REVELATION 19:11-16, 19-21

28th Seven Praises

I will give thanks to the Lord with my whole heart.
I will tell of all your marvelous works.
I will be glad and rejoice in you.
I will sing praise to your name, O Most High.

Psalm 9:1-2

THE SOVEREIGN CREATOR OF ALL

I bless you, O Most High,
    I praise and honor you, who live forever.
Your dominion is an everlasting dominion,
    and your kingdom from generation to generation.
All the inhabitants of the earth are regarded as nothing;
    you do according to your will with the army of heaven,
    and among the inhabitants of the earth.
No one can stop your hand,
    or ask you, "What are you doing?"

Whatever you do, it shall be forever. Nothing can be added
to it, nor anything taken from it; you have done it, that men
should fear before you.

Ancient of Days, you take your seat on the throne.
Your clothing is white as snow,
    and the hair of your head like pure wool.
Your throne is ablaze with fire,
    its wheels aflame.
A river of fire flows out from before you.
    Thousands of thousands minister to you.
    Ten thousand times ten thousand stand before you.

Jesus, there came with the clouds of the sky
    One like a Son of Man.
You came to the Ancient of Days,
    and you were presented before him.
Dominion was given you,
    and glory, and a kingdom,
That all the peoples, nations, and languages
    should serve you.
Your dominion is an everlasting dominion,
    which will not pass away.
Your kingdom will never be destroyed.

ECCLESIASTES 3:14; DANIEL 4:34-35; 7:9-10, 13-14

PSALMS

I give thanks to you, Lord, for you are good;
  your lovingkindness endures forever.
I give thanks to the God of gods;
  I give thanks to the Lord of lords,
  to you alone who do great wonders.
  Your lovingkindness endures forever.
By your understanding you made the heavens;
  you spread out the earth above the waters.
You made the great lights,
  the sun to rule by day,
  the moon and stars to rule by night.
  Your lovingkindness endures forever.
You struck down the Egyptian firstborn
  and brought out Israel from among them,
  with a strong hand, and with an outstretched arm.
You divided apart the Red Sea
  and made Israel pass through the middle of it,
  but you overthrew Pharaoh and his army in the Red Sea.
  Your lovingkindness endures forever.
You led your people through the wilderness,
  and struck great kings,
  and killed mighty kings,
  and gave their land as an inheritance,
  even a heritage to Israel your servant.
  Your lovingkindness endures forever.
You give food to every creature.
  Your lovingkindness endures forever.
I give you thanks, O God of heaven;
  for your lovingkindness endures forever.

I praise you, Lord,
  even you who made heaven and earth.
Your hands have made me and formed me.
  I am yours.
I hope in you, Lord, from this time forward and
   forevermore.

PSALM 119:73, 94; 131:3; 134:1, 3; 136:1-26

THE LOVING AND FAITHFUL GOD

You are the Lord, the God of all flesh. Is there anything too
hard for you? You are the one who does it. You form the
plans to establish it. I AM THAT I AM is your name. You say,
"'Call to me, and I will answer you, and will show you great
and mysterious things, which you don't know."

Lord, you have healed my waywardness.
> You have loved me freely.
You are the one who answers and takes care of me.
> Your ways are right.
> The righteous walk in them.

You are the LORD my God, gracious and merciful,
> slow to anger and abundant in lovingkindness,
>> relenting from sending calamity.

Lord, surely you have done great things.
> I won't be afraid.
I will be glad and rejoice, for you have done great things.
> I will be glad and rejoice in you.
> You will restore to me the years that the swarming locust
>> has eaten.
I will be satisfied, and will praise your name, O Lord my
> God.
> You have dealt wondrously with me;
> your people will not be disappointed.
I know that you are with me.
> You are the Lord my God, and there is no one else;
> I will not be disappointed.
You have poured out your Spirit on all flesh;
> sons and daughters prophesy.
> Old men dream dreams.
> Young men see visions.
On your servants you have poured out your Spirit.

Lord, you roar from Zion,
> and thunder from Jerusalem;
> the heavens and the earth shake;
> but you are a refuge to your people,
> a stronghold to us.

JEREMIAH 32:27; 33:2-3; HOSEA 14:4, 8-9; JOEL 2:13, 20-29; 3:16

FATHER, SON, SPIRIT

Jesus, you are the image of the invisible God, the firstborn of all creation.

By you are all things were created in the heavens and on the earth, visible and invisible, whether thrones or dominions or principalities or powers. All things have been created through you and for you.

You are before all things, and in you all things are held together.

Jesus, you are the head of the body, the Church. You are the beginning, the firstborn from the dead, that in all things you might have the supremacy.

The Father was pleased for all of his fullness to dwell in you, and through you to reconcile all things to himself, whether things on the earth or things in the heavens, having made peace through the blood of your cross.

God's mystery, which he hid from past ages and generations, but has now revealed, is this: you in us.

You are the mystery of God. In you are hidden all the treasures of wisdom and knowledge.

You are the head, from whom all the body, being supplied and knit together through the joints and ligaments, grows with God's growth.

You are the head over all principalities and powers.

Your power works mightily within me.

You forgave me. You gave yourself for my sins to deliver me out of this present evil age.

I give thanks to the Father through you.

Jesus, in you there is neither Greek nor Jew, circumcision nor uncircumcision, barbarian, slave, or free person; but you are all, and in all.

I praise you!

GALATIANS 1:4; COLOSSIANS 1:15-20, 23, 26-27, 29; 2:2-3, 10; 2:19; 3:11, 13, 17

CHRIST'S VICTORY

Jesus, I praise you that you are the author of my salvation. You made atonement for my sins.

Because of the suffering of death, which you tasted for me, you were crowned with glory and honor. You sat down at the right hand of the majesty in the heavens.

Jesus, you were made perfect through your sufferings. You were made perfect forever. Having been made perfect, you became my source of eternal salvation.

Father, you made a promise to Abraham, and I am an heir of that promise.

Because of your unchangeable purpose and your unchangeable oath, I have a sure and steadfast hope. It is impossible for you to lie.

That hope is the anchor of my soul.

Jesus, you went in, past the veil, as my forerunner. You are my high priest forever.

You are exactly the high priest I needed: holy, innocent, undefiled, separated from sinners, and exalted above the heavens.

You don't need to offer up sacrifices daily. Rather, you offered a sacrifice once for all, to put away sin, when you offered up yourself.

You guarantee a covenant better than the old one. The law appointed priests who were weak because they died, but the Father's oath appointed you, his Son.

Jesus, since you live forever, you hold your priesthood permanently. So you can save to the uttermost all of us who draw near to God through you. You make intercession for me forever.

I praise you!

HEBREWS 2:9-10, 17; 5:9; 6:13-14, 17-20; 7:24-28; 8:1

PSALMS

Lord, I will give you thanks with my whole heart.
 Before the gods I will sing praises to you.
I will bow down and give thanks to your name
 for your lovingkindness and for your truth;
 for you have exalted your name and your word above all.
In the day that I called, you answered me.
 You encouraged me with strength in my soul.
All the kings of the earth will give you thanks, Lord,
 for they have heard the words of your mouth.
Yes, they will sing of your ways,
 for your glory is great!
For though you are on high, yet you look after the lowly;
 but you know the proud from afar.
Though I walk in the middle of trouble,
 you will revive me.
You will stretch out your hand against the wrath of
  my enemies.
 Your right hand will save me.
You will fulfill that which concerns me.
 Your lovingkindness, Lord, endures forever.

You are my hiding place and my shield.
 I hope in your word.
Your word is a lamp to my feet,
 and a light for my path.

All of your words are truth;
 my heart stands in awe of your words.
I rejoice at your word, Lord,
 as one who finds great plunder.
Let my lips utter praise,
 let my tongue sing of your word.

Lord, I praise you!

PSALM 119:105, 119, 160, 162, 171, 172; 129:4; 138:1-8

THINGS TO COME

Jesus, after you reign with your faithful witnesses for a thousand years, Satan will be released from his prison, and will deceive the nations of the earth and gather them together for war. They will surround the camp of the saints, and their beloved city.

But fire will come down out of heaven from God and devour them.

The devil who deceived them will be thrown into the lake of fire and sulfur, where the beast and the false prophet will be also. They will be tormented day and night forever and ever.

Jesus, John saw a great white throne, and him who sat on it, from whose face earth and heaven fled away. No place was found for them.

The dead, the great and the small, stood before the throne, and they opened books.

Another book was opened, the book of life. The dead were judged out of the things which were written in the books, according to their works.

The sea gave up the dead who were in it. Death and Hades gave up the dead who were in them. They were judged, each one according to his works.

Death and Hades were thrown into the lake of fire. That is the second death. If anyone was not found written in the book of life, he was cast into the lake of fire.

Righteous Judge, I praise you!

REVELATION 20:4, 7-15

29TH SEVEN PRAISES

I will give thanks to you, Lord, among the peoples.
I will sing praises to you among the nations.
Be exalted, God, above the heavens!
Let your glory be over all the earth!

PSALM 57:9, 11

THE SOVEREIGN CREATOR OF ALL

Lord, you are the living God;
    you endure forever.
Your kingdom will never be destroyed.
    Your dominion will have no end.
You deliver and rescue.
    You perform signs and wonders in heaven and in earth.

The kingdom, the dominion, and the greatness of the kingdoms
    under the whole sky will be given to your holy ones,
        O Most High.
Your kingdom is an everlasting kingdom,
    and all dominions will serve and obey you.

You, Most High, rule in the kingdom of men. You give it to
whomever you will.

You are the Lord of heaven. The gods of silver, gold, bronze,
iron, wood, and stone don't see, or hear, or know. I glorify you,
in whose hand my breath is, and who holds all of my ways.

O Lord my God, you are righteous in all your works which
you do.

Lord, you are the God of hosts;
    I AM THAT I AM is your name of renown!

You are the one who forms the mountains,
    and creates the wind,
    and declares your thoughts to man.
You make the morning darkness,
    and tread on the high places of the earth.
I AM THAT I AM, the God of Armies, is your name.

Lord, you made the Pleiades and Orion,
    and turn the darkness into the morning,
    and make the day into night;
    you summon the waters of the sea,
    and pour them out on the surface of the earth.
I AM THAT I AM is your name.

DANIEL 4:25; 5:23; 6:26-27; 7:27; 9:14; HOSEA 12:5; AMOS 4:13; 5:8

PSALMS

Lord, you have searched me, and you know me.
You know my sitting down and my rising up.
    You perceive my thoughts from afar.
You search out my path and my lying down,
    and are acquainted with all my ways.
Before there is a word on my tongue, Lord,
    you know it altogether.
You hem me in behind and before.
    You have laid your hand on me.
This knowledge is too wonderful for me.
    It's too high; I can't attain it.
Where could I go from your Spirit?
    Or where could I flee from your presence?
If I ascend up into heaven, you are there.
    If I make my bed in Sheol, you are there!
If I take the wings of the dawn,
    and settle in the uttermost parts of the sea,
Even there your hand will lead me,
    and your right hand will hold me.
If I say, "Surely the darkness will overwhelm me.
    The light around me will be night,"
Even the darkness doesn't hide from you,
    but the night shines as the day.
    The darkness is like light to you.
You formed my inmost being.
    You knit me together in my mother's womb.
I give thanks to you, for I am fearfully and wonderfully made.
    Your works are wonderful; my soul knows that very well.
My frame wasn't hidden from you, when I was made in secret,
    woven together in the depths of the earth;
    your eyes saw my body.
In your book they were all written,
    the days that were ordained for me,
    when as yet there were none of them.
How precious to me are your thoughts, God!
    How vast is their sum!
If I would count them, they are more in number than the sand.
    When I wake up, I am still with you.

PSALM 139:1-18

THE LOVING AND FAITHFUL GOD

I called out to you, Lord, because of my affliction.
    You answered me.
Out of the belly of Sheol I cried.
    You heard my voice.
O Lord my God, you have brought up my life from the pit.
    When my soul fainted within me, I remembered you.
    My prayer came to you.
Salvation belongs to you, Lord.
    I will sacrifice to you with the voice of thanksgiving.
Lord, you are gracious and compassionate, slow to anger
    and abundant in lovingkindness,
    and one who relents concerning calamity.

All the nations may walk in the name of their gods;
    but I will walk in the name of the Lord my God forever
        and ever.
Lord, you rescue me.
    You redeem me from the hand of my enemies.
Who is a God like you, who pardons iniquity,
    and passes over the disobedience of the remnant of
        your people?
You don't stay angry forever,
    because you delight in lovingkindness.

Lord, though the fig tree doesn't flourish,
    nor fruit be in the vines;
    the labor of the olive fails,
    the fields yield no food;
    the flocks are cut off from the fold,
    and there is no herd in the stalls:
    yet I will rejoice in you.
    I will be joyful in the God of my salvation!
Lord, you are my strength.
    You make my feet like deer's feet,
    and enable me to go in high places.

JONAH 2:2, 6-9; 4:2; MICAH 4:5, 10; 7:18; HABAKKUK 3:17-19

FATHER, SON, SPIRIT

Lord Jesus Christ, you are glorious!

You are my only Master, God, and Lord. I always rejoice in you! In everything I give thanks to you!

You are Lord. Your grace is with me. May your name be glorified in me, and me in you, according to your grace and the grace of the Father.

You are the Lord of peace. You are my hope. In you are faith and love.

Your grace toward me is more than abundant. You gave yourself as a ransom for all. You are the one mediator between God and man. I have believed in you for eternal life.

Jesus, in you is the promise of life. Grace is in you.

You are the offspring of David, risen from the dead. In you is salvation with eternal glory.

I was redeemed, not with corruptible things, with silver or gold, but with precious blood, as of a lamb without blemish or spot—your blood.

You raised me with you. You are seated at the right hand of God. I died, and my life is hidden with you in God. When you, who are my life, are revealed, I will be revealed with you in glory.

My Lord and my Savior, you are faithful.

Thank you for every good thing that is in me, for your sake.

Jesus, you are full of humility and gentleness. Through you I have obtained mercy.

I praise you for your grace, that though you were rich, yet for my sake you became poor, that through your poverty I might become rich.

I am yours. In your liberty I have been made free.

Come, Lord Jesus! Your grace is always with me.

1 CORINTHIANS 16:22-23; 2 CORINTHIANS 4:1; 8:9; 10:1, 7; GALATIANS 5:1; COLOSSIANS 3:1-4; 1 THESSALONIANS 5:16, 18, 28; 2 THESSALONIANS 1:12; 3:16, 18; 1 TIMOTHY 1:1, 14, 16; 2:5; 2 TIMOTHY 1:1; 2:1, 8, 13; TITUS 1:4; PHILEMON 1:6; JAMES 2:1; 1 PETER 1:18-19; JUDE 1:4

CHRIST'S VICTORY

Jesus, you are my high priest. You sat down at the right hand of the throne of the Majesty in the heavens.

You are the mediator of a new, far better covenant, which you have ushered in with far better promises:

> "I will put my laws into their mind,
>   I will also write them on their heart.
> I will be their God,
>   and they will be my people.
> They will not teach every man his fellow citizen,
>   and every man his brother, saying, 'Know the Lord,'
>   for all will know me,
>   from their least to their greatest.
> For I will be merciful to their unrighteousness.
>   I will remember their sins and lawless deeds
>   no more."

I praise you, Lord!

Jesus, under the old covenant gifts and sacrifices were offered. But they couldn't make the worshipper perfect in conscience.

Your law was only a shadow of the good things to come, and not the substance.

So it could never make perfect those who drew near. It couldn't take away sins, or the consciousness of sins. The Law's sacrifices just reminded people of their sins year after year.

But you, Jesus, offered one sacrifice for sins forever and sat down at the right hand of God.

Through your one offering, the offering of your body once for all, you have perfected me forever.

ROMANS 16:27; HEBREWS 8:1, 6, 10-12; 9:9, 15; 10:1, 2, 11, 12, 14

Psalms

Blessed be you, Lord, my rock.
　　You train me for battle.
You are my lovingkindness, my fortress,
　　my high tower, my deliverer, my shield.
　　You are the one in whom I take refuge.
I will sing a new song to you, God.
　　I will sing praises to you.
You are the one who gives salvation.
　　I am happy to have you as my God.

I praise you, Lord.
　　Praise the Lord, O my soul.
While I live, I will praise you.
　　I will sing praises to my God as long as I have my being.
I am happy because I have you, God, for my help;
　　my hope is in you,
Who made heaven and earth,
　　the sea, and all that is in them;
　　you keep truth forever.
Lord, you execute justice for the oppressed;
　　you give food to the hungry.
You free the prisoners.
　　You open the eyes of the blind.
　　You raise up those who are bowed down.
　　You love the righteous.
You preserve the foreigners.
　　You uphold the fatherless and widow,
　　but you turn the way of the wicked upside down.
Lord, you will reign forever;
　　you are God to all generations.
I praise you, Lord!

Psalm 144:1-2, 9-10, 15; 146:1-2, 5-10

THINGS TO COME

Jesus, there will be a new heaven and a new earth: for the first heaven and the first earth will pass away, and the sea will be no more.

The holy city, New Jerusalem, will come down out of heaven from God, prepared like a bride adorned for her husband.

God, your dwelling will be with people. You will dwell with us, and we will be your people.

You yourself will be with us as our God.

You will wipe away every tear from our eyes.

Death will be no more; neither will there be mourning, nor crying, nor pain, anymore. The first things will have passed away.

Father, you who sit on the throne say, "Behold, I am making all things new."

Your words are faithful and true.

You are the Alpha and the Omega, the Beginning and the End.

You will give freely to him who is thirsty from the spring of the water of life.

He who overcomes, you will give him these things. You will be his God, and he will be your son.

I praise you!

REVELATION 21:1-7

30TH SEVEN PRAISES

My tongue shall declare Your righteousness
And Your praise all day long.

PSALM 35:28, NASB

THE SOVEREIGN CREATOR OF ALL

Lord, you are the God who commands armies.
You touch the earth and it melts;
    all who live on it will mourn.
You build your rooms in the heavens
    and have established your vault on the earth.
You summon the waters of the seas
    and pour them out on the surface of the earth.
I AM THAT I AM is your name.

You are slow to anger but great in power;
    you will by no means allow the wicked to go unpunished.
You go out in the whirlwind and in the storm;
    the clouds are the dust of your feet.
You rebuke the sea and make it dry.
    You dry up all the rivers.
The mountains quake before you,
    and the hills melt away.
The earth trembles at your presence,
    the world and all who dwell in it.
Who can stand before your indignation?
    Who can endure the fierceness of your anger?
Your wrath is poured out like fire,
    and you break apart the rocks.
But you are good, Lord;
    you are a stronghold in the day of trouble.
You know those who take refuge in you.

Lord, you stretch out the heavens, and lay the foundation of
the earth. You form the spirit of man within him.

You are awesome to us. Men will worship you, everyone
from his place, even all the shores of the nations.

From the rising of the sun even to its going down, your
name is great among the nations, and in every place. You are
the Lord of hosts!

AMOS 9:5-6; NAHUM 1:3-7; ZECHARIAH 12:1; ZEPHANIAH 2:11; MALACHI 1:11

PSALMS

I will exalt you, my God, the King.
  I will praise your name forever and ever.
Every day I will praise you.
  I will extol your name forever and ever.
Great are you, Lord, and greatly to be praised!
  Your greatness is unsearchable.
One generation will commend your works to another,
  and will declare your mighty acts.
I will meditate on the glorious splendor of your majesty,
  on your wondrous works.
I will speak of the might of your awesome acts and will
      declare your greatness.
  I will utter the memory of your great goodness,
  and will sing of your righteousness.
Lord, you are full of compassion and mercy,
  slow to anger, and great in lovingkindness.
You are good to all; your tender mercies are over all your works.
  All your works will give thanks to you, Lord.
  Your saints will extol you.
They will speak of the glory of your kingdom,
  and talk about your power,
  to make known to the sons of men your mighty acts,
  the glory of the majesty of your kingdom.
Your kingdom is an everlasting kingdom.
  Your dominion endures throughout all generations.
You are faithful in all your words, and loving in all your deeds.
  You uphold all who fall, and raise up all those who are
      bowed down.
Lord, you are righteous in all your ways,
  and gracious in all your works.
You are near to all those who call on you,
  to all who call on you in truth.
You will fulfill the desire of those who fear you.
  You also will hear their cry, and will save them.
You preserve all those who love you,
  but all the wicked you will destroy.
My mouth will speak your praise, Lord.
  Let all flesh bless your holy name forever and ever.

PSALM 145:1-14; 17-21

THE LOVING AND FAITHFUL GOD

Lord, out of Bethlehem would come from you
      one to be ruler in Israel;
   his goings forth would be from of old,
   from days of eternity.
She who was in labor would give birth.
Jesus, you would arise, and shepherd in the strength of
      the Lord,
   in the majesty of the name of the Lord your God.
   Your flock would live, for you would be great to the
      ends of the earth.
You are our peace.

Lord, the daughter of Zion rejoices greatly.
   The daughter of Jerusalem shouts.
You, the King, come to us!
   You are righteous, and endowed with salvation;
   lowly, and riding on a donkey,
   even on a colt, the foal of a donkey.
You will speak peace to the nations:
   and your dominion will be from sea to sea,
   and from the River to the ends of the earth.

Jesus, you would pour on David's house, and on the
inhabitants of Jerusalem, the spirit of grace and of
supplication.

They would look on you whom they pierced, and they
would mourn for you, as one mourns for his only son,
and would grieve bitterly for you, as one grieves for his
firstborn.

Lord, you are my God.
   I acknowledge none but you.
   Besides you there is no savior.

I praise you, Jesus!

HOSEA 13:4-6; MICAH 5:2-5; ZECHARIAH 9:9-10; 12:10-14

FATHER, SON, SPIRIT

Jesus, you are the Father's Son. When you came into the world, all the angels of God worshipped you.

Your throne, O God, is forever and ever.
>The scepter of uprightness is the scepter of your kingdom.

You have loved righteousness and hated iniquity;
>therefore God, your God, has anointed you with the oil of gladness above your companions.

You, Lord, in the beginning, laid the foundation of the earth.
>The heavens are the works of your hands.

They will perish, but you continue.
>They all will grow old like a garment.

You will roll them up like a mantle,
>and they will be changed;
>but you are the same.
>Your years will not end.

Jesus, when you purified me of my sins, you sat down at the right hand of the Majesty on high.

You are the one who sanctifies me. You are not ashamed to call me your brother, because I am one of the children God gave you.

You are faithful as a Son over God's house. I am part of that house.

You came to do the Father's will. I praise you that by that will I have been sanctified through the offering of your body once for all. By your blood I am sanctified.

Jesus, you are the author and perfecter of my faith. For the joy set before you, you endured the cross, despising its shame, and you sat down at the right hand of the throne of God.

You are the same yesterday, today, and forever.

Through you I continually offer up a sacrifice of praise to God, the fruit of my lips that give thanks to his name.

HEBREWS 1:3-6, 8-12; 2:11, 13; 3:1, 6; 10:9-10, 29; 12:2; 13:8, 15

CHRIST'S VICTORY

Jesus, you came as a high priest of the coming good things.

You didn't enter the holy place made with hands, but rather the greater and more perfect tabernacle, not made with hands, and not of this creation. You entered heaven itself to appear in the presence of God for me.

You offered yourself without blemish to God. You didn't enter through the blood of goats and calves, but through your own blood.

You entered once for all into the holy place, having obtained eternal redemption.

You put away sin by the sacrifice of yourself.

By your blood, Jesus, by the way you inaugurated for me, I have boldness to enter the holy place. Through your flesh you opened a new and living way through the veil.

You are the great high priest over God's house.

So I can draw near with a sincere heart, being fully assured in my faith, with my heart sprinkled clean from an evil conscience.

Through you, Jesus, I can hold fast the confession of my hope without wavering, because you who promised are faithful.

Jesus, I praise you that you are the mediator of a new covenant. Commandments about eating and drinking and festivals and Sabbath days were a shadow of the things to come. You are the reality!

Your blood cleanses my conscience from dead works to serve the living God, so I might receive the promise of the eternal inheritance.

I praise you!

COLOSSIANS 2:16-17, 22; HEBREWS 9:11-12, 14-16, 24, 26; 10:19-23

PSALMS

I praise you, Lord,
>   for it is good to sing praises to my God;
>   it is pleasant and fitting to praise you.
You heal the brokenhearted,
>   and bind up their wounds.
You count the number of the stars.
>   You call them all by their names.
Great are you, Lord, and mighty in power.
>   Your understanding is infinite.
You uphold the humble.
>   You bring the wicked down to the ground.
I sing to you, Lord, with thanksgiving.
>   I sing praises to my God.
You cover the sky with clouds;
>   you prepare rain for the earth;
>   you make grass grow on the mountains.
You provide food for the livestock,
>   and for the young ravens when they call.
The eyes of all wait for you.
>   You give them their food in due season.
You open your hand,
>   and satisfy the desire of every living thing.
You don't delight in the strength of the horse.
>   You take no pleasure in the legs of a man.
You take pleasure in those who fear you,
>   in those who hope in your lovingkindness.
You send out your commandment to the earth.
>   Your word runs very swiftly.
You give snow like wool,
>   and scatter frost like ashes.
You hurl down your hail like pebbles.
>   Who can stand before your cold?
You send out your word, and melt them.
>   You cause your wind to blow, and the waters to flow.
I praise you, Lord!

PSALM 145:15-16; 147:1-20

THINGS TO COME

Jesus, you are the Lamb. Your bride, the holy city, Jerusalem, will come down out of heaven from God, having the glory of God.

Its light will be like a most precious stone, as if it were a jasper stone, clear as crystal.

It will have a great and high wall, with twelve gates, and at the gates twelve angels; and names written on them, which are the names of the twelve tribes of the children of Israel. The wall of the city will have twelve foundations, and on them twelve names of the twelve Apostles of the Lamb.

The city will be pure gold, like pure glass. It will be 1500 miles long and wide and high.

There will be no temple in it, for the Lord God, the Almighty, and you, the Lamb, will be its temple.

The city will have no need for the sun or moon to shine, for the very glory of God will illuminate it, and you will be its lamp.

The nations will walk in its light. The kings of the earth will bring the glory and honor of the nations into it.

Its gates will not be shut by day (for there will be no night there), and they will bring the glory and the honor of the nations into it so that they may enter. Only those who are written in the Lamb's book of life will enter.

Lamb of God, I praise you!

REVELATION 21:9-12, 14, 16, 18, 22-27

31st Seven Praises

Praise the Lord!
Praise God in his sanctuary!
Praise him in his heavens for his acts of power!
Praise him for his mighty acts!
Praise him according to his excellent greatness!
Let everything that has breath praise the Lord!
Praise the Lord!

Psalm 150:1-2, 6

THE SOVEREIGN CREATOR OF ALL

Lord God, my Holy One, you are from everlasting. As the
waters cover the sea, the earth will be filled with the knowledge
of your glory. You are in your holy temple. Let all the earth be
silent before you!

I stand in awe of your deeds, Lord.
> In wrath, you remember mercy.
> You are the Holy One.

Your glory covers the heavens,
> and your praise fills the earth.

Your splendor is like the sunrise.
> Rays shine from your hand, where your power is hidden.

Plague goes before you,
> pestilence follows behind you.

You stood and shook the earth.
> You looked and made the nations tremble.

The ancient mountains were crumbled,
> the age-old hills collapsed.
> Your ways are eternal.

Lord, you uncovered your bow.
> You called for your sworn arrows.
> You split the earth with rivers.

The mountains saw you, and were afraid.
> The storm of waters passed by.
> The deep roared and lifted up its hands on high.

The sun and moon stood still in the sky,
> at the light of your arrows as they went,
> at the shining of your glittering spear.

You marched through the land in wrath.
> You threshed the nations in anger.

You went out for the salvation of your people,
> for the salvation of your anointed.

Lord, you have ascended up into heaven, and descended.
> You have gathered the wind in your fists.

You have bound the waters in your garment.
> You have established all the ends of the earth.

I know your name, and your Son's name.

PROVERBS 30:4; HABAKKUK 1:12; 2:14, 20; 3:1-6, 9-13

Psalms

Praise the Lord!
    Praise the Lord from the heavens!
    Praise him in the heights!
Praise him, all his angels!
    Praise him, all his army!
Praise him, sun and moon!
    Praise him, all you shining stars!
Praise him, you highest heavens,
    and you waters that are above the heavens.
Let them praise your name, Lord,
    for you commanded, and they were created.
You have established them forever and ever.
    You have made a decree which will not pass away.
Praise the Lord from the earth,
    you great sea creatures, and all depths;
Lightning and hail, snow and clouds;
    stormy wind, fulfilling his word;
Mountains and all hills;
    fruit trees and all cedars;
Wild animals and all livestock;
    small creatures and flying birds;
Kings of the earth and all peoples;
    princes and all judges of the earth;
Both young men and maidens;
    old men and children:
Let them praise your name, Lord,
    for your name alone is exalted.
    Your glory is above the earth and the heavens.
You have lifted up the horn of your people,
    the praise of all your saints.
I praise you, Lord!

Psalm 148:1-14

The Loving and Faithful God

Lord, I look to you.
> I will wait for the God of my salvation.
> My God will hear me.

Don't rejoice over me, my enemy.
> When I fall, I will arise.
> When I sit in darkness, Lord, you will be a light to me.

You will bring me out to the light.
> I will see your righteousness.

Lord, you are righteous, doing no wrong.
> Every morning you bring your justice to light.
> You never fail.

You have removed all judgment from me.
> You have thrown out my enemy.
> I will not be afraid anymore.

My King, the God of Armies, is with me.
> You are a warrior who delivers.

You take great delight in me.
> You quiet me in your love.
> You rejoice over me with singing.

Lord, you strengthen me and save me.
> You have mercy on me.

You are my God, and you hear me.
> You strengthen me in yourself,
> and in your name I will walk.

You refine me as silver is refined.
> I call on your name, and you hear me.

You say, "You are mine,"
> And I say, "You are my God."

To those who fear your name,
> the sun of righteousness will arise with healing in
> > its wings.

Lord, you have loved me.
> I am yours, your treasured possession.

Micah 7:7-9; Zephaniah 3:5, 15-17; Zechariah 10:6, 12; 13:9; Malachi 1:2; 3:17; 4:2

Father, Son, Spirit

Jesus, you are the living stone, rejected by men, but choice and precious to God. You are the stone which the builders rejected, but you have become the chief cornerstone.

You came to take away my sins. In you there is no sin. I am sprinkled by your blood.

Though I don't see you now, yet believe in you, I rejoice greatly with joy that is unspeakable and full of glory.

Because I believe in you, Lord, I will not be disappointed.

I am healed by your wounds. You are the Shepherd and Overseer of my soul.

You suffered for my sins once, the righteous for the unrighteous, that you might bring me to God. You were put to death in the flesh, but made alive in the Spirit.

God raised you from the dead and gave you glory. You are at the right hand of God, having gone into heaven. Angels and authorities and powers have been made subject to you.

You were foreknown before the foundation of the world, but you were revealed in this last age for our sake—those who believe in God through you. So my faith and hope are in God.

In all things, may God be glorified through you. To you belongs the glory and the dominion forever and ever! Your kingdom is an eternal kingdom.

Jesus, I have obtained a precious faith by the righteousness of you, my God and Savior.

Your disciples were eyewitnesses of your majesty on the mountain. You received honor and glory from God the Father when the Majestic Glory said from heaven, "This is my beloved Son, in whom I am well pleased."

My Lord and Savior, through the knowledge of you I escape the defilement of the world. Through you I overcome the world.

To you be the glory, both now and forever!

1 Peter 1:2, 8, 20-22; 2:4-7, 24-25; 3:18, 21-22; 4:11; 2 Peter 1:1, 11, 16-17; 2:20; 3:18; 1 John 3:5; 5:4-5

CHRIST'S VICTORY

I praise you, God and Father of my Lord Jesus Christ!
You have blessed me with every spiritual blessing in the
heavenlies in Christ.

Thank you for choosing me in Christ before the foundation
of the world, that I would be holy and blameless before you.

Father, in your love, you predestined me to be adopted as
your child through Jesus Christ to yourself. That was the
good pleasure of your will. May the glory of your grace be
praised!

Father, I praise you that, in Jesus, your beloved, you freely
showered your grace on me.

Jesus, in you, I am redeemed through your blood.

Father, my sins have been forgiven according to how
incredibly rich your grace is—the grace you lavished on me.

In all of your wisdom and insight, you made known to us
the mystery of your will. You did this according to the plan
you established in Christ. You'll bring it to pass when the
time is right.

Your plan is this: that all things would be united in Christ,
under his authority—both the things in the heavens and the
things on the earth.

Father, you have given me an inheritance in Christ. You
predestined me for this according to your purpose, because
you work all things according to the counsel of your will.

That makes me, who have hoped in Christ, a praise to the
glory of your grace!

Father, when I heard the word of the truth, the good news of
your salvation, and I believed, you sealed me in Christ with
the promised Holy Spirit.

Holy Spirit, you are the pledge of my inheritance until I, God's
possession, am fully redeemed—all to the praise of his glory.

Father, Son, and Spirit, I praise you!

EPHESIANS 1:3-14

Psalms

I praise you, Lord!
I sing to you a new song,
    your praise in the assembly of the saints.
I rejoice in you, my Maker;
    I am joyful in my King.
I praise your name with the dance;
    I sing praises to you with tambourine and harp!
For you take pleasure in me, Lord.
    You crown me with salvation.
I am joyful in glory;
    I sing for joy on my bed.
The high praises of you, God, are in my mouth,
    and a two-edged sword in my hand,
To bind kings with chains,
    and nobles with fetters of iron;
    to execute the written judgment.
All your saints have this honor.
    I praise you, Lord!

I praise you, Lord!
    I praise you in your sanctuary!
    I praise you in your heavens!
I praise you for your mighty acts of power!
    I praise you according to your excellent greatness!
Praise God with the sounding of the trumpet!
    Praise him with harp and lyre!
Praise him with tambourine and dancing!
    Praise him with stringed instruments and flute!
Praise him with loud cymbals!
    Praise him with resounding cymbals!
Let everything that has breath praise you, Lord!
    I praise you, Lord!

Psalm 149:1-9; 150:1-6

THINGS TO COME

Jesus, a river of the water of life, clear as crystal, will proceed out of the throne of God and of the Lamb, down the middle of the street of the new Jerusalem.

On either side of the river will be the tree of life, bearing twelve kinds of fruits, yielding its fruit every month. The leaves of the tree are for the healing of the nations.

There will no longer be any curse.

The throne of God and of the Lamb will be in it, and your servants will serve you. We will see your face, and your name will be on our foreheads.

There will be no night, and we will need no lamp light or sunlight; for the Lord God will illuminate us. We will reign forever and ever.

Jesus, you are the Alpha and the Omega, the First and the Last, the Beginning and the End. You are the root and offspring of David, the Bright and Morning Star.

Holy Spirit, you and the bride say, "Come!" Anyone who hears can say, "Come!" Whoever is thirsty may come. Whoever wants can take the water of life freely.

Jesus, you say, "Yes, I am coming quickly."

Amen! Yes, come, Lord Jesus.

REVELATION 22:1-5, 13, 16, 17, 20-21

ABOUT DAVID GREGORY

The New York Times' extended bestselling author David Gregory has enthralled readers with "what-if" stories involving unexpected, life-changing encounters in seven novels, including *Dinner with a Perfect Stranger*, with over half a million copies sold, and Christy Award finalist *The Last Christian*. Three of his books have been made into feature films. David has also authored two nonfiction books, *The Rest of the Gospel: When the Partial Gospel Has Worn You Out* and *If Jesus Loves Me Why Isn't This Working?* A native of Texas, David holds master's degrees from Dallas Theological Seminary and The University of North Texas. He was formerly on the ministry team of Insight for Living, the Bible-teaching ministry of Charles Swindoll.

For more information about David, to invite him to speak, or to simply connect with him, find him at:

www.davidgregorybooks.com

 **facebook.com/DavidGregoryAuthor**

twitter.com/davidgregorybooks

OTHER BOOKS
BY DAVID GREGORY

Dinner with a Perfect Stranger: An Invitation Worth Considering

A Day with a Perfect Stranger

Night with a Perfect Stranger: The Conversation That Changes Everything

The Rest of the Gospel: When the Partial Gospel Has Worn You Out (with Dan Stone)

If Jesus Loves Me Why Isn't This Working?

The Last Christian: A Novel

Open: Get Ready for the Adventure of a Lifetime

Patriot Rules: A Novel

The Next Level: A Parable of Finding Your Place in Life